ADVERTISING

WHAT EVERYONE NEEDS TO KNOW®

ADVERTISING

WHAT EVERYONE NEEDS TO KNOW®

MARA EINSTEIN

OXFORD
UNIVERSITY PRESS

OXFORD
UNIVERSITY PRESS

Oxford University Press is a department of the University of Oxford.
It furthers the University's objective of excellence in research, scholarship,
and education by publishing worldwide. Oxford is a registered trade mark of
Oxford University Press in the UK and certain other countries.

"What Everyone Needs to Know" is a registered trademark of
Oxford University Press.

Published in the United States of America by Oxford University Press
198 Madison Avenue, New York, NY 10016, United States of America.

Library of Congress Cataloging-in-Publication Data
Names: Einstein, Mara, author.
Title: Advertising : what everyone needs to know / Mara Einstein.
Description: New York, NY : Oxford University Press, [2017] |
Includes bibliographical references and index.
Identifiers: LCCN 2016038612 (print) | LCCN 2016051488 (ebook) |
ISBN 9780190625894 (pbk. : alk. paper) | ISBN 9780190625887 (cloth : alk. paper) |
ISBN 9780190625900 (pdf) | ISBN 9780190625917 (ebook)
Subjects: LCSH: Advertising–Social aspects. | Advertising.
Classification: LCC HF5821 .E395 2017 (print) |
LCC HF5821 (ebook) | DDC 659.1—dc23
LC record available at https://lccn.loc.gov/2016038612

1 3 5 7 9 8 6 4 2

Paperback printed by LSC Communications, United States of America
Hardback printed by Bridgeport National Bindery, Inc., United States of America

To my daughter, Cayla, who has enriched my world beyond measure and for whom anything is possible.

CONTENTS

Chapter 3. Consumer Behavior 55

Chapter 5. Advertising and Society 117

Chapter 6. Media: Advertising's Everywhere 149

Chapter 7. Advertising in the Digital Age   181

ADVERTISING

WHAT EVERYONE NEEDS TO KNOW®

INTRODUCTION

Three thousand. Some have even said five thousand.

That's the number of marketing messages the average American confronts on a daily basis. True, we are not aware of all of those communications, which come from everything from packaging to television commercials to native advertising within our Facebook newsfeeds, but that does not mean we are not affected by them. They influence the clothes we buy, the cars we drive, the coffee we drink. Think about it. Are you Starbucks or Dunkin' Donuts? Subaru or Lexus? Budweiser or Heineken? It is very likely you have a preference and not simply because of what the products are but because of the brand images and mythologies embedded in them—ideas that have become associated with these products through advertising and other forms of promotion. And as we use these products, they become building blocks for our personalities. Some people are Apple, some are PC, for example, and this idea is translated into advertising with phrases starting with "I am": I am Mac. I am FedEx. I am Vera Bradley. This is, of course, not simply an American phenomenon. Multinational corporations and digital technologies have expanded consumerism and its concomitant commercial messages around the world.

Advertising is not new. Criers—merchants calling out their wares—were the earliest form of advertising. Gutenberg's printing press was instrumental in expanding advertising during the fifteenth century. With the advent of mass production during the Industrial Revolution of the eighteenth and nineteenth centuries, advertising moved from selling locally crafted works to selling vast quantities of products. By the late nineteenth and early twentieth centuries, manufacturers began to brand their products with the hope that consumers would ask for a specific type of cookie (say an Oreo) over a generic sandwich cookie. At the same time, the century ushered in what historian T.J. Jackson calls the "therapeutic ethos," which suggested that product purchases could provide not only gratification through having bought a product but also fulfillment and peace of mind for having done so. This is key: advertising shifted from a focus on attributes (physical features) to benefits (what the customer receives). So, for example, in the 1950s Marlboro cigarette commercials were not simply about a good smoke but about a cowboy and the rugged individualism he represented. This continues today with millennials (young adults born from the early 1980s to 2000) being treated to fun and adventures associated with the brand, a new twist on advertising called experiential marketing whereby we no longer passively interact with a brand communication but rather are fully immersed in a brand experience. It is rare nowadays to find a product that is sold via a straightforward explication of the product benefits. Rather, most advertisers sell products and services by appealing to our emotions, particularly within the online environment. That is because it is intense emotions—particularly awe and anger—that are most likely to lead us to share marketing messages with others. We have seen this in campaigns from the Ice Bucket Challenge, to marketing camouflaged as extreme sporting events brought to you by Red Bull, to heart-wrenching videos like "Sketch Artist" from Dove, and female empowerment videos such as "Like a Girl" from Always.

Every day—and now because of digital technologies, twenty-four hours a day—people are assaulted with advertising. These marketing messages come in a variety of formats: TV commercials, magazine and newspaper print ads, radio commercials, pop-up ads on gaming apps, pre-roll on YouTube videos, native advertising on mobile news apps—the list goes on and on. While you have likely become adept at avoiding advertising, particularly on television through DVRs or online with ad blockers, the truth is that advertisers have become decidedly adept at finding new ways to put advertising in front of you—so much so that it is often difficult to discern the difference between an ad and a news article, a legitimate recommendation or a paid Influencer tweet.

Advertising is pervasive. We are exposed to marketing messages practically from the time we are born. Maternity wards are target-rich environments for selling Pampers and baby formula. But it doesn't stop there. Schools sell class rings, sure, but they also sell soda and junk food and sneakers. McDonald's even has "McTeacher" nights. Corporate brands provide schools with classroom kits meant to facilitate learning, but the vast majority of them contain biased material, thus hindering clear critical thinking.[1] Increasingly, companies use a cradle-to-grave strategy that hooks us into their products at a young age and keeps us ensnared throughout our lives. Think here of Disney. Disney promotes its Disney Baby division to moms with newborns in maternity wards. Kids are targeted from the time they can interact with an iPad. School-aged kids are the target for Club Penguin and the Disney Channel. Brides are invited to have a magic Cinderella wedding, and parents and grandparents are targets for Disney theme parks and all they have to offer to their offspring. Note, too, that advertising is no longer limited to toothpaste or laundry soap. It is used to sell any number of social and cultural institutions, from religion to philanthropy to higher education. Really, it is hard to think of an area where marketing has not had some effect.

1. *Campaign for a Commercial Free Childhood* (n.d.). Marketing in Schools Fact Sheet. Retrieved May 10, 2016 from http://www.commercial freechildhood.org/sites/default/files/schools.pdf.

This book will help you to understand how the advertising and marketing industries work. More important, it will help you to understand its subtle and not-so-subtle impact on your life. This is particularly important today because it has become almost impossible to separate ourselves from the missives of the marketplace. In addition, since media (and with it marketing) change so quickly and many of the concepts attached to it are made purposefully vague and opaque by the industry, this book will be an especially helpful guide for those trying to understand advertising in the digital age. It is a book that is in conversation with the many others on the market about big data. The use and manipulation of vast quantities of data is only a small part of the issue. More relevant here is understanding what information is being communicated and to what end. The truth is we tend to forget that the Internet is—first and foremost—an advertising platform. It is not about you posting your vacation pictures for your friends and family to see on Facebook, for example. It is about how marketers can sell you your next vacation. Finally, as more and more advertising (and more and more advertising dollars) moves out of so-called legacy media like TV and newspapers and moves into digital, the likelihood increases that we will have to pay more and more money for our media content—because we didn't live up to the implicit agreement of advertising: we will sit through biased commercial messages in order to get the content for free.

1

FROM ADVERTISING TO MARKETING

What is advertising?

Advertising is a paid communication used to persuade someone to buy a product or service of an identified sponsor. The advertisement is disseminated through media and can be in the form of a print ad (magazine, newspaper, or outdoor), a radio or television commercial, or a digital ad, which can be either static or video-based. Each type of advertising is best suited for a different marketing purpose. Thirty-second television commercials are useful in evoking emotion because of their use of sight and sound. Print advertising is effective if the product needs considerable explanation, in the case of life insurance for example, or if an advertiser wants people to have a chance to look at a product in more detail, say clothing or a diamond ring. Outdoor advertising reminds consumers about a product in order to keep it "top of mind"—that is, in your awareness so you will remember to buy it when you are in the store. And, after all, it would be difficult to convey scads of information when someone is driving down the highway at sixty miles per hour. In all of these cases, the message is created to appeal to a specific, defined group of people known as the target audience. In sum, the job of the advertising is to get the right message to the right person at the right time and place.

When most people think about being sold to by a company, they think of advertising. They consider what car to buy because of a commercial they saw on television or they try Mr. Clean Magic Erasers because of an ad they saw in a magazine. In the best of all corporate worlds, that is how advertising is supposed to work. In truth, it is far more complex than that. Advertising is part of a much larger business function—that is, marketing. While we may not be conscious of all the ways that marketers work to tempt us with their goods, we are aware of advertising.

Do all companies or organizations use advertising?

In a word, yes. Given all the communications clutter, organizations of all types—for profit or nonprofit, private or public—need to advertise in order to be part of the cultural conversation. And because digital media have driven down the price of advertising, there is no reason for a company not to advertise.

This is not to say that all advertisers are equal or equally visible to us in the marketplace. We are most aware of categories that spend heavily across media platforms. Consumer package goods (CPG) companies, like Procter & Gamble and Unilever, use advertising to sell everything from Tide to Crest to Axe. Telecommunications (AT&T, Verizon, Sprint) and car manufacturers (notably General Motors, Ford, and Fiat Chrysler) are also big spenders. Other categories include cosmetics (L'Oreal, Maybelline, CoverGirl), entertainment (Disney, Fox, Marvel), retail stores (Walmart, Target, Macy's), as well as electronics, beer, soda, pharmaceuticals, and so on and so on. Beyond tangible items, advertising promotes services such as banking, restaurants, and local bicycle repair stores. More broadly, advertising is used to promote social and cultural ideas like politics (and political candidates), religion, education, and the arts. We will look at the implications of commercialization and consumerism on these institutions throughout the book.

How do they come up with the ideas for advertising?

In a traditional advertising agency, there are four major departments that work together to create advertising that is informative and entertaining and will appeal to the target audience: account management, research or account planning, creative, and media.

The account management group oversees everything that has to do with the brand. They are in daily contact with the advertiser (the client), and they are charged with knowing the business of their client almost as well as the client does. It is their job to know how much product is sold, whether sales are going up or down, who the competitors are, and what major issues are affecting or may in the future affect product sales or the product category overall. All of this is necessary because advertising exists to solve a business problem, which could be simply to increase sales or introduce a product or, more difficult, to change people's perception about a brand. Let's take an example: in the athletic apparel category Nike has historically dominated the segment. Lately, however, they have been experiencing serious competition from upstart Under Armour. Under Armour has made a number of smart strategic business and marketing decisions that have led to them now being number two in the category. First, the company had been known primarily for men's athletic apparel. To increase sales, they broadened their product line to include clothing for women, focused on producing footwear as well as apparel, and produced a series of ads that targeted women, notably an online one with supermodel Gisele Bündchen and another traditional commercial with Misty Copeland, principal dancer for the American Ballet Theatre, that appeared during the Super Bowl. The commercials used the tagline, "I will what I want," a concept that is in line with women's empowerment messages that are so popular of late. Second, Under Armour purchased a number of fitness apps, including MyFitnessPal and Endomondo, giving the company access to diet and workout data about millions of active, health-conscious people. In doing this, Under Armour moved from a little-known athletic company to a ubiquitous fitness and technology company and a considerable threat to Nike in the marketplace. Because of these actions on the part of Under Armour, the Nike account team became tasked with developing a strategy to retain their number one position. Should Nike get current users to use their product more? Should they try to steal consumers back from Under Armour? Can they get people who've never gotten off the couch to believe they can be athletes and need to buy workout apparel, particularly in an Olympic year?

This is where research, or account planning, comes in. Knowing what is going on from a business perspective is market research, what we have been discussing thus far. *Marketing* research is information that enables advertisers to understand what consumers think about their product (or their competitor's product) and how they engage with it. If Under Armour users are diehard fans, for example, trying to get them to switch is an uphill battle and probably not a strategy Nike should pursue. In order to determine this, the research department will need to develop an understanding of their consumer through a combination of research methodologies (these will be discussed at length in Chapter 3 on consumer behavior). Historically, the research department relied on surveys to understand what consumers want. One of the earliest researchers in this area was George Gallup, famously of the Gallup Polls. Today this department is often called Account Planning, a concept that came out of the United Kingdom. Rather than being a number cruncher, the account planner is someone who becomes the voice of the consumer in the advertising process, letting the creative team know whether the work they are developing would resonate with the target consumer. This information is derived through interacting with consumers, which can be done through focus groups (groups of ten to twelve people led by a moderator to answer questions about their use of a product category and brands), one-on-one interviews, or ethnographies, where researchers immerse themselves with consumers in their home or other environment where they might use a product, such as researching vodka usage by attending bars or in-home parties. While these methodologies will continue to be used, big data is changing the way that much research is being done, with more and more information being derived from analyzing online purchase behavior.

Based on the work of the account team and the account planner, the creative department will come up with a series of advertising concepts. The ideas are developed by dyads made up of an art director and a copywriter. They report to a creative director who oversees the work of the account overall. This is important because on larger accounts there may be multiple campaigns, and all ad campaigns must work in a unified way. After a few ideas are sketched out, they will be shown to the creative director, who will comment on them and ask for changes as necessary. Then the work will be shown to the account team (who will also make comments) and if all are in agreement, the work will be presented to the client. Once the client approves, the advertising will be produced.

Simultaneously, the media group will be planning the best place to put the advertising message. A number of elements must be taken into consideration. When is the best time to advertise in terms of time of year, time of day, and day of the week? Nike might want to advertise in January when people are making New Year's resolutions; Taco Bell will advertise in the morning as people are running out the door to go to work to remind them of their breakfast offerings; and movie companies advertise on Thursday night because people are making their weekend plans. What types of media should be used? Most companies use a combination of media types, called the *media mix*. This will include television (broadcast and cable), radio, magazines, newspapers, outdoor ads, and online. Who is the target audience? Through research, the target audience will have been defined in terms of age and gender as well as product usage and lifestyle. If the advertiser is trying to reach women who are concerned about health and fitness, they might advertise in *Self* magazine or *Women's Health*. More specifically, the target group might be women trying to get back into shape after having a baby, so then the ads might appear in *Parenting* or *Working Mother*. The environment where the advertising will appear is important because the message needs to work in conjunction with what appears around it. Media departments work assiduously to make sure this happens. It is no coincidence when a raisin ad appears next to a recipe for oatmeal raisin cookies or a Beats headphones ad appears next to a Top 10 list of the best electronics, which may well include Beats among the recommended products to purchase.

Is there more than one type of advertising?

The most prominent form of advertising is consumer or brand advertising. These are what we typically think of when we think of advertising: ads for Chevrolet, Cheerios, or Crest toothpaste. Business-to-business is advertising where one company is promoting its product to another company, perhaps American Airlines promoting its coast-to-coast flights to the entertainment industry or credit card companies selling their services to colleges who in turn promote the cards on campus. Public service announcements (PSAs) are ads that promote a social initiative such as dissuading people from illegal drug use ("This is drugs. This is your brain on drugs.") or railway safety (Australia's very amusing "Dumb Ways to Die"). These ads are often produced pro bono and the media space is provided for free. Direct response advertising provides a means through which the consumer can contact the advertiser directly, typically through an 800 number; long-form infomercials are included in this category. Finally, corporate advertising promotes the company or corporation overall, rather than an individual product or brand. These ads are produced by the corporate communications (public relations) department rather than the marketing department and are targeted to Wall Street investors or other opinion leaders the company wants to influence, like government officials. However, if the company has done something particularly egregious, a corporate ad might be produced to win back public opinion. A good example here is when Volkswagen apologized for lying to the public and the government about compliance with emission standards.[1]

Is there a difference between advertising and marketing?

Most definitely. Advertising is a form of communication used to persuade people to buy. Marketing is a coordinated strategy to engender desire within consumers for a particular brand by managing the relationship between the consumer and the brand as well as creating value for the consumer—that is, us. It is one of only three major areas within a corporation, the other two being operations and administration. Marketing, however, is the area responsible for generating sales.

Marketing encompasses four elements: product, price, place, and promotion, commonly called the *marketing mix* or the 4Ps.

The first P—product—entails everything that has to do with the physical object or service being sold. First and foremost, it is the attributes associated with the product. If the company is selling a car, how fast does it go, are there leather seats, what are the safety features? Or for toothpaste—is it paste or gel, does it whiten or protect against tartar, is it safe for kids? Or think here of the white headphones that come with an iPod or iPhone. At the time of the product's introduction, this was an important design element that enabled the product to stand

---

1. Dante D'Orazio (November 15, 2015), "Volkswagen Apologizes for Emissions Scandal with Full-Page Ad in Dozens Of Papers," *The Verge*. Retrieved April 14, 2016 from http://www.theverge.com/transpor tation/2015/11/15/9739960/volkswagen-apologizes-with-full-page-ad-in-dozens-of-newspapers.

out from its competitors, all of whom included black headphones with their devices. The advertising exploited this difference by creating ads that focused attention on it. You may remember early ads that used a bright color in the background, with a black silhouette of a young person listening to music, and the one element that fairly popped off the page was the white headphones that didn't just hang down from the ear but seemed to dance across the page. The account team looks for distinguishing elements like this to promote in the advertising. Beyond physical attributes, the product's name, its packaging, and the logo, tagline, and other branding elements all play into how consumers relate to a product and ultimately how it will be advertised.

Price is what we pay for a product. How a product is priced is a strategic decision, not simple arithmetic. Henry Ford, for example, priced the Model T to be widely affordable in order to advance the profitability of mass production. Today, magazines charge very little for a subscription because they want to create a large audience for advertisers. Margin—the difference between the selling price and the cost of goods—does factor into pricing decisions. However, it is only one element. Apple, for example, keeps margins high by charging more than its competitors and can do so because of consumer loyalty to its products. Starbucks, too, charges a premium price for its products. (It has been estimated high-end coffee drinks have an 80 percent markup.[2]) Finally, pricing plays into our perceptions about a product. Higher-priced products are perceived to be of higher quality, whether that is true or not. Marketers can get away with generating significant margins as long as we see value for the money. High-end cosmetics is a good example here.

---

2. Quentin Fottrell (December 6, 2012), "What Starbucks' $7 Coffee Is Really Worth," *MarketWatch*. Retrieved May 10, 2016 from http://www.marketwatch.com/story/what-starbucks-7-coffee-is-really-worth-2012-11-29.

Place is where and how the product is sold, what marketers call the distribution channels. Products are sold in different places with varying levels of availability and these choices, too, communicate information about the product to consumers. Some products—like candy, gum, and cigarettes—are widely available, thus using an extensive distribution strategy. We pick these items up on the go with little forethought, so it is best to put them in as many places as possible. Other products will be more exclusive, and it is that exclusivity that makes us willing to pay a premium. Clothing designers like Prada or Kate Spade are good examples here, as are high-end electronics such as Harmon Kardon.

Promotion entails the various ways in which a company stimulates desire for its products. This includes consumer promotions and sweepstakes, rebates, personal selling, direct marketing, public relations, events, loyalty programs, and, of course, advertising. Not all of these elements will be used in every category. Personal selling—one-on-one, face-to-face selling—is very expensive so is limited in its use. Pharmaceutical marketing to doctors is one category where this is widely used. Loyalty programs are typically associated with airline frequent flyer programs or retail stores (if you have a CVS or a Stop & Shop card on your key ring, then you are part of a loyalty program). Public relations—influencing or persuading the public—is used by most brands and has been gaining in popularity on digital media. Advertising, then, is a subset of the broader field of marketing. It is one element in the marketer's tool kit, but a very important one, as it sets the tone for interactions between the company and its consumers.

What is the difference between public relations and advertising?

Public relations is concerned with managing the reputation of a company, a brand, or a person. PR practitioners attempt to positively affect perceptions among key stakeholders for a company, including employees, local communities, and shareholders, not just consumers. Key to their job is creating and maintaining relationships with the media (i.e., journalists). That is because much of their work entails generating publicity, either by writing press releases, creating video press kits, or pitching story ideas. Importantly, those journalists are not compelled to write about what the PR person is selling. Say the new season of *Game of Thrones* is about to launch. HBO will put together a press kit with a press release, pictures of the cast, and pictures from "behind the scenes," and will provide some short footage from the show, perhaps including interviews with some of the stars. This content will be made available to news outlets, including TV writers at newspapers and daytime and evening talk shows as well as TV news outlets. Actors from the show will be made available to appear on *The Late Show with Stephen Colbert* and *Ellen* and so on. Video will also be seeded on YouTube and different methods will be used to generate discussion throughout social media. Journalists and talk shows are likely to write about or use this content because they know it will be interesting to readers and viewers. The same cannot be said if P&G comes out with a new laundry detergent. Unless there is some very compelling aspect of that product, the press does not have to write about it. Therefore, the company will turn to advertising—that is, paying to get their message out to the public.

This is the key difference between advertising and public relations: advertising is paid for and PR is not. Because companies pay for placement, the advertising must run. With PR, there are no guarantees. However, because PR is not paid for, there is an implied third-party endorsement, and with that PR garners more credibility with readers. We know when we read an ad that there is a biased, self-serving corporation behind it. When we read an article about a product, our guard is down because we believe the piece to be written by an unbiased source.

PR, however, is not simply about publicity and media relations. It is about community affairs, financial relations, crisis management, and even lobbying.

Why has public relations become so central to marketing?

Social media have fundamentally changed public relations. Traditionally, public relations dealt with "controlled media" and "uncontrolled media." Controlled media are tools like annual reports, industrial films, or staged events. Uncontrolled media are talk shows or stories that are pitched to journalists. With social media, uncontrolled media have gotten, well, out of control. Anyone can comment—often negatively—about a company, making reputation management similar to playing Whack-a-Mole. A plane is delayed and people run to Twitter to complain. With readily available video on cellphones, YouTube has become a hotbed of discontent. There are several well-known examples of fast food workers complaining about their jobs through videos showing them taking a bath in the sink at work or playing with food in disgusting ways before serving it to a customer.

Companies have learned how to manage consumer (and employee) discontent and to use the digital space to their advantage. Increasingly, companies participate in real-time listening to learn what people are saying about them online as it is happening. Yes, they respond to positive comments, but also they insert themselves into negative conversations in order to manage the communications and ultimately their reputation. Brands from Gatorade to JetBlue to Nike to Purina have done particularly well at this. In my research, I have heard marketers say, "Social is for social, not for selling," the idea being that social media are for developing relationships with individual consumers (which is known as customer relationship marketing but has its roots in PR). So rather than mass marketing or niche marketing, what we have today is a move toward more and more one-on-one interactions with consumers. This is why many believe PR may overtake advertising as the more prominent promotional tool.

Lastly, online there is what is known as paid, owned, and earned. Paid media is advertising; owned media are company websites, blogs, and social media pages; and earned media is publicity that has been gotten for free (i.e., PR). Companies strive to increase earned media to support owned media so they don't have to spend a lot of money on paid media. We will examine this in more depth in Chapter 6.

What is branding?

According to advertising legend David Ogilvy, a brand is "the intangible sum of a product's attributes: its name, packaging, and price, its history, its reputation and the way it is advertised." A brand, then, has little to do with the product itself and everything to do with what we think about it.[3]

Look around. From Horizon milk in your fridge to Starbucks coffee on every corner, from your iPhone in your hand to the Honda in your driveway, from your Gap jeans to the JetBlue credit card in your wallet, there are few places where you won't see a branded product. And, if you are a parent, you have been confronted with the practically herculean task of trying to find a t-shirt or lunch box without the latest Disney star or Nickelodeon cartoon character.

3. For information on branding, see Douglas Holt, *How Brands Become Icons: The Principles of Cultural Branding* (Boston: Harvard Business School Press, 2004); Adam Arvidsson, *Brands: Meaning and Value in Media Culture* (London: Routledge, 2006); Celia Lury, *Brands: The Logos of the Global Economy* (London: Routledge, 2004); Marcel Danesi, *Brands* (New York: Routledge, 2006); James Twitchell, *Branded Nation: The Marketing of Megachurch, College Inc., and Museumworld* (New York: Simon and Schuster, 2004); Albrecht Rothacher, ed., *Corporate Cultures and Global Brands* (Singapore: World Scientific, 2004); Gareth Williams, *Branded? Products and Their Personalities* (London: V & A, 2000); Robert Goldman and Stephen Papson, *Sign Wars: The Cluttered Landscape of Advertising* (New York: Guilford, 1996); and for criticism see Naomi Klein, *No Space, No Choice, No Jobs, No Logo: Taking Aim at the Brand Bullies* (New York: Picador, 2000).

Why is branding so pervasive?

Why turn a pair of TOMS shoes into a statement about philanthropy, or a soap product like Dove into a promoter of women's empowerment?

Because we relate to products that have meaning attached to them. Marketers tell stories about their products through promotion, whether it be advertising or public relations or Facebook posts. These narratives, called *brand mythologies*, work in combination with the company logo and possibly a tagline to enable consumers to instantaneously associate the product with the story when they see the logo.[4] The goal is for ideas and emotions around a product to be elicited in a split second.

Let's take an example. Fundamentally, Red Bull is a foultasting energy drink chockfull of caffeine and sugar. But is that what you think about when you see the skinny, silver metal can with the bull on it? Of course not. You think of extreme sports and yet-to-be-discovered rock bands and guys jumping out of rockets from outer space. But why? Why isn't Red Bull just a means for quenching your thirst or helping you stay awake during finals week or an all-nighter at work? Because branding has created a tale for you about what that energy drink is and what it can do for you—specifically, it enables you to think that you might experience those extreme adventures.

4. Not all academics or marketers agree, but there is increasing research suggesting that brands may be less influential in identity production than initially believed. See Holt, *Branding* (2004) and Z. Arsel and C. Thompson (2011), "Demythologizing Consumption Practices: How Consumers Protect Their Field-Dependent Identity Investments from Devaluing Marketplace Myths," *Journal of Consumer Research* 37(5): 791–807. Also Robert Kozinets and Jay Handelman (2004), "Adversaries of Consumption: Consumer Movements, Activism, and Ideology," *Journal of Consumer Research* 31(3): 691–704; J. D. Rumbo (2002), "Consumer Resistance in a World of Advertising Clutter: The Case of Adbusters," *Psychology & Marketing* 19(2): 127–148; V. Carducci (2006), "Culture Jamming: A Sociological Perspective," *Journal of Consumer Culture* 6(1): 116–138.

Through numerous YouTube videos, endless online advertising, sponsorships (including video gaming events known as eSports and producing the Red Bull Music Academy), sampling (putting mini Red Bull trucks just outside the gates of college campuses), and word of mouth, Red Bull has established a mythology around their products. So much so that some might even say that mythology has generated a cult following.

Beyond the myth, there is the logo and the tagline. The logo is a bright yellow circle with two red bulls with their horns pointed toward one another as if they are in a bull ring, all on a blue background. The product packaging is also iconic, with an eye-catching blue-and-silver checkerboard pattern on a can that is smaller and slimmer than a typical soda can. The Red Bull logo goes beyond the energy drink product. It exists on magazines and at music festivals, on Red Bull TV and at Red Bull sporting events. To further embed product information in the minds of consumers, Red Bull uses the tagline "Red Bull Gives You Wiiings." All this is done so that anyone who sees the logo will think "risk-taking."

In other examples, we see Cinderella's castle with the Disney logo and Tinkerbell and we think "magic." Or, we see the swoosh and we think "Nike ... innovation ... inspiration," and the Coca-Cola logo evokes happiness. Remember, we see thousands of messages a day. The only way for a product company to "break through the clutter" is to be meaningful to us—and quickly.

Branding communicates ideas through a consumer product. Through advertising and marketing a physical object is endowed with meaning and the product—now a brand—becomes more than the sum of its parts. With the new shared meaning created by the consumer engaging with the product, a personal connection is made between the consumer and the product (or service), which leads to thoughts and feelings that have nothing to do with the product's physical attributes. We buy brands that fulfill a need, either physical or psychological. Dove is not merely a body wash but a way to feel good about one's self. AT&T allows us to communicate with others but more importantly it is about how to "Reach out and touch someone," so that friends and family become our focus when we purchase these phones and services rather than how good (or bad) the network is. So whether it is self-assurance or personal connections, the goal is to have us connect these experiences and emotions with the product. Over time, as you have more and more positive interactions with the brand, the more likely you are to purchase it over and over again.

One final thing to note: branding is random. It is a made-up tale used to sell a product. David Ogilvy also said, "I could have positioned Dove as a detergent bar for men with dirty hands, but chose instead to position it as a toilet bar for women with dry skin." Same is true for that stalwart of masculine brands, Marlboro. The product was originally targeted to women and the brown filter was used to hide lipstick stains. However, when soldiers came back from World War II, famous Chicago ad man Leo Burnett decided to boost sales by reframing the product as a way for war heroes to assert their masculinity, individuality, and rugged American spirit by associating the brand with an icon that embodied these ideals: the cowboy known as the Marlboro Man. Rebranding this cigarette is a great example of how products in and of themselves have no meaning. The brand—the logo, the mythology, the meaning—is the product. The soap or the cigarette is secondary.

Why is branding so important to consumers?

Brands become part of our identity. They help us define who we are to ourselves as well as those around us. What we wear, the phone we carry, the car we drive are all identifiers that tell others who we are.[5] Marketers talk about this as "brands as badges." So you may think one thing about someone with a

---

5. For information about possessions and sense of self see R. Belk (1988), "Possessions and the Extended Self," *Journal of Consumer Research* 15(2):139–168; A. Ahuvia (2005), "Beyond the Extended

can of Budweiser in their hand, but have a completely different perception of that person if you replaced that Bud can with a bottle of Heineken. This is all due to branding. The same idea applies to cars, clothes, and cosmetics. In the past, we might have been defined by our religion or our jobs or our family. Today, this is no longer true. Our religions are fungible, our jobs are "permalance," and divorce rates are sky high. Filling in the space for these institutions are corporate brands that have the stability that these old-time institutions no longer have. While our jobs may not last, McDonald's French fries will be the same in Tulsa and Toronto and Tampa.

And, because brands have become so much a part of who we are, we expect them to be embedded with the values that we hold dear. It is a rare advertisement that will tell you the attributes (the physical aspects of a product) and benefits (what the product will do, such as get your clothes whiter) without also telling you how buying the product is somehow related to making the world a better place.

Branding is so much a part of our environment that personal branding—turning ourselves into brands—has become the norm. Personal branding is driven by a number of factors. First, the increasingly freelance job market requires that laborers be able to distinguish themselves. Second, social media are driven by influencers—people who influence others to buy. Getting more followers on Twitter and friends on Facebook is the currency of the day, and the way to drive those numbers

Self: Loved Objects and Consumers' Identity Narratives," *Journal of Consumer Research* 32(1): 171–184; B. Mittal (2006), "I, Me, and Mine—How Products Become Consumers' Extended Selves," *Journal of Consumer Behavior* 5(6): 550–562; E. Goffman, *The Presentation of Self in Everyday Life* (New York: Doubleday, 1959); M. Csikszentmihalyi and E. Rochberg-Halton, *The Meaning of Things: Domestic Symbols and the Self* (Cambridge, UK: Cambridge University Press, 1981); and G. McCracken, *Culture and Consumption: New Approaches to the Symbolic Character of Consumer Goods and Activities* (Bloomington: Indiana University Press, 1988).

is through self-promotion. Finally, just like the Marlboro Man, people relate to people more than products, so brands connected to people drive interest. Think here of (God help me) the Kardashians. Also, Steve Jobs and Apple, Richard Branson and Virgin, and the YouTube or Vine "stars" like PewDiePie, Jenna Marbles, and Lele Pons.

What is the goal of advertising?

That depends on whose perspective you are looking at.

Consumers want two things from advertising: entertainment and information. Advertising must be entertaining to grab our attention. Informationally, advertising must be relevant. If it isn't, we won't even notice it because we naturally screen out unnecessary content. You know what I mean if you have ever been in the market for a car. As soon as you start shopping, it seems like everywhere you look there are car commercials. Where did they all come from? Truth is, they were always there, but you naturally shut them out.

Companies want to sell us their products. Period.

How do advertisers get us to buy their products?

Several different strategies will be used to get us to buy. For new products, marketers want to motivate us to try their product, so the job is to advertise it as much as possible to get the word out. With an established product, marketers will either want us to try it again (reminder advertising), or they may try to get existing consumers to use their product more. A good way to do this is to provide new uses. Arm & Hammer Baking Soda is a good example. After women entered the job market en masse in the 1960s and there was less time for baking, the company promoted using the product to keep the freezer and refrigerator smelling clean—and to change the box every three months. Or when women starting earning significant salaries and getting married later, the diamond industry started selling diamond rings to women, claiming that the left hand is for "we" and the right is for "me."

Branding is used to differentiate one product from another. This is particularly important today because so many products are commodities—that is, one product is really not that different from another. Creating preferences for one brand over another enables marketers to lure customers away from the competition with the goal to turn users into fans and maybe even "brand evangelists" and lifetime users. Companies don't want you to buy a six-pack of Budweiser, they want you to be a lifelong "Bud drinker." It's the difference between $10 and tens of thousands of dollars.

Can advertisers get us to buy a product that we don't want?

History would tell us no. One of the biggest product failures of all time was the Ford Edsel. This car was heavily promoted, the company claimed to have done product research, and yet after seeing it, customers said a big "no thank you." Ford's failure was so spectacular that subsequent marketing campaign disasters are often called Edsels.

Edsel's story helps explain the value of the 4Ps. When a product does not sell, a marketer has to evaluate each element to discover where something is going wrong. In this case, the promotion did its job. People went in droves to check out the Edsel. The problem was the pricing and the product; the cost confused consumers about what car class it was supposed to be and, worse, the car was flat-out ugly.

On the other hand, some might argue that we bought Pet Rocks. True enough, and this should lead you to think back to branding: the company embedded a mythology into a product that turned it into a fad, making the product something people "had to have."

Marketers can manipulate us and push us toward buying things we don't need. Check out your closet and see how many clothes you have with tags still on them or how many plastic cartons you had to buy from The Container Store to hold all the things you never use. Reality shows about hoarders abound and, frankly, work like diet shows—we can look at someone's overstuffed house and think, "I'm not that bad."

As you know more about how advertising and marketing work, you can begin to resist its siren's call even when it comes to inexpensive purchases like Pet Rocks. Part of what should hearten you is knowing that you cannot really be duped into buying something, even by the most sophisticated of marketers. Apple Watch, anyone? I didn't think so.

2

THE BUSINESS
OF ADVERTISING

What is the economic impact of advertising?

Advertising affects virtually every product category. You would be hard pressed to find a computer, book, toothpaste, shampoo, spaghetti sauce, or jar of mayonnaise that has not been marketed to you, save for perhaps the store's generic brands, and even those are now often promoted for the larger chain stores like Target and Stop & Shop. Advertising costs are embedded into the price of the products we buy, which means we pay for the privilege of having these products sold to us.

And pay we do. Here are the statistics. In 2014, advertising influenced spending on $5.8 trillion in U.S. sales. Producing those ads are a growing cadre of marketing professionals. There were 142 million advertising jobs in 2014, which was up 14 percent from the year before. Salaries and wages totaled $1.9 trillion, or approximately 17 percent of all U.S. labor income.[1] In sum, advertising is very big business.

---

1. Katie Richards (November 17, 2015), "Ad Industry Accounted for 19 Percent of U.S. GDP in 2014: New Findings from ANA and The Advertising Coalition," *Adweek*. Retrieved May 10, 2016 from http://www.adweek.com/news/advertising-branding/study-ad-industry-contributed-nearly-20-percent-toward-us-gdp-2014-168164.

How much money is spent on advertising in the United States?

The 2016 forecast for advertising spending on media in the United States is expected to reach $190 billion. However, if we add marketing services to that, the number jumps to $420 billion, or $1298 per person.[2] This is why marketing is so important to understand. Yes, advertisers are putting messages in front of you on television and in magazines and online, but they are also tempting consumers through sales promotions, telemarketing, direct mail, event sponsorship, directories, and public relations. But that's not all. These numbers only take into account measured media. Increasingly there are corporate messages appearing within media content (product placement) or surreptitiously online (content marketing) that are not included in these figures.

What about worldwide spending?

Worldwide, advertising spending is estimated to be $519.8 billion. Including marketing spending, that number jumps to $965.1 billion—close to one *trillion* dollars. By region, media ad spending is the largest in North America ($187.6 billion), followed by Asia Pacific ($173.4 billion), Western Europe ($94 billion), Latin America ($32 billion), Middle East and Africa ($18.2 billion), and Central and Eastern Europe ($12.4 billion).[3] The world's largest advertising markets in order by spending are the United States, China, Japan, the United Kingdom, Brazil, Germany, France, Australia, Canada, and South Korea. The United States is the biggest by far with $178 billion in spending, more than twice that of second-place China ($85.5

2. *Advertising Age* (December 21, 2015), "Marketing Fact Pack: 2016 Edition," p. 14. Retrieved April 13, 2017 from http://gaia.adage.com/images/bin/pdf/20151211marketingfactpackweb.pdf.
3. The discrepancy between the North American spending figure and the U.S. one is only due to these numbers being estimates from two different advertising companies. The difference accounts for about 5 percent.

billion). Japan, in third place, spends less than half of that of China ($38.6 billion).[4]

America's disproportionate advertising spending has had considerable consequences for the United States, from childhood obesity to gender stereotyping to environment destruction. As other countries increase their advertising expenditures and witness the growth in corporate multinationals fueled by neoliberal philosophies, these issues of consumerism are being exported overseas.

Who is the biggest advertiser?

Procter & Gamble (P&G) is the world's undisputed largest advertiser. Annual spending figures, however, vary. It is estimated that in 2015, the company spent $4.6 billion in the United States and somewhere between $8 and $11 billion worldwide.[5] Spending is applied across four product categories: beauty; health and grooming; fabric and home care; and baby, feminine, and family care. Within these consumer segments are dozens of famous household brands, including Pantene and Old Spice; Crest and Pepto-Bismol; Tide laundry detergent and Dawn dishwashing liquid; and finally, Pampers, Charmin, Tampax, and Always.[6] The company has a long history of being a leader in marketing and advertising, having long emphasized research in order to provide consumers with "new news," an idea related to the unique selling proposition (USP) whereby advertisers repeated a message to consumers over and over again. This concept was fundamental in the 1950s at the time of the rise of mass media and its concomitant mass marketing. P&G was the first company to advertise

4. *Advertising Age* (December 21, 2015), "Marketing Fact Pack: 2016 Edition," p. 15. Retrieved April 14, 2017 from http://gaia.adage. com/images/bin/pdf/20151211marketingfactpackweb.pdf.
5. *Adbrands*, "P&G Profile." Retrieved April 10, 2016 from http://www. adbrands.net/us/pg_us.htm.
6. To see a full listing of P&G's brands: http://us.pg.com/our_brands.

nationally to consumers (starting in the 1880s), and the company was the creator of the "soap opera," first in radio and then in television, as a way to target female consumers. While the company spends significantly in television (the most expensive form of advertising), P&G has stated that they are moving money away from this medium and into digital platforms. P&G (as well as other mega-brand company Unilever, maker of Dove, Lipton Tea, and Hellman's Mayonnaise, among others) plans to spend 30 to 35 percent of its budget online.[7] In 2016, one of the world's largest ad-buying companies, Magna Global, announced that it would be moving $250 million of its clients' advertising budgets out of traditional television and into YouTube.[8] When the largest advertiser and one with a conservative approach to marketing shifts its advertising spending out of television and media firms are shifting significant ad dollars out of legacy media, it is going to have a ripple effect across the industry. We have not seen the full impact of this yet, but expect that we will within the next few years.

In the meantime, P&G produces smart, sophisticated, and effective marketing campaigns using a combination of digital and traditional media. Campaigns that come to mind are "The man your man wants to be" for Old Spice and cosmetic brand CoverGirl's tie-in with movies like *The Hunger Games* and *Star Wars* and TV shows like *Empire*, which enable the company to tap into young as well as multiethnic audiences. P&G has long been a sponsor of the Olympics, and their 2014 "Thank You Mom" campaign is a case study in how to integrate online and

7. Jack Neff (April 20, 2015), "Brutal TV Upfront Ahead as Buyers, Sellers Toughen Bargaining Positions," *Advertising Age*, p. 4.
8. Jim Rutenberg (May 15, 2016), "When TV Ads Go Subliminal with a Vengeance, We'll Be to Blame," *New York Times*. Retrieved May 16, 2016 from http://www.nytimes.com/2016/05/16/business/media/when-tv-ads-go-subliminal-with-a-vengeance-well-be-to-blame.html?ribbon-ad-idx=4&rref=business/media&module=Ribbon&version=context&region=Header&action=click&contentCollection=Media&pgtype=article&_r=0.

offline advertising. P&G started with an online video called "Best Job" that highlights the joys of motherhood. This was followed by television commercials featuring mothers doing the work of supporting their children in their Olympic dream. To support these promotions, the company paid for product placement (also called an *integrated segment*) on NBC's *The Today Show*. A document from P&G's advertising agency states: "Throughout the broadcast, the cast referenced the online popularity of 'Best Job,' aired the full 2-minute version within programming and additionally aired the: 60 version in the 'A' position during the commercial break. The pièce de résistance was a P&G executive appearing on the show to surprise moms of Olympians with a financial gift to help them get to London (based on the insight that many families couldn't afford the trip)."[9] Online, P&G gave all mothers an opportunity to rave about their kids on social media by creating a Thank You Mom Facebook page and a Twitter handle (@ThankYouMom), helping create emotional connections with the company. Athletes with considerable followings posted thanks to their moms, and YouTube videos—some with footage provided by NBC, which agreed to secure shots of athletes' moms as part of the promotion—captured heartwarming moments of moms reacting to the wins and losses of their athletic offspring. This integrated online and offline initiative was the most successful campaign in Procter & Gamble's 175-year history, leading to incremental sales of $200 million, a considerable feat for well-established brands. It is not surprising, then, that they brought the campaign back for the 2016 Summer Olympics, launching the campaign just before Mother's Day.

Like any company, P&G has had its share of product flops and marketing missteps. In the 1970s, the company produced Touch of Yogurt shampoo, which confused some consumers

9. Advertising Education Foundation (n.d.), "Medaling In Media: P&G Proud Sponsor of Mom." Retrieved April 20, 2015 from http://www.aef.com/pdf/jay_chiat/2013/p&g_olympic_proud-sponsor.pdf.

enough that they ate it instead of using it on their tresses. More recently, the company came under attack for its Tide Pods. This laundry product—small packets of detergent in a clear plastic tub—looked like candy in a candy jar and children were being poisoned because they ingested the product. P&G was loath to eliminate the product because Tide is one of its iconic brands and it accounts for $3 billion in annual sales (out of P&G's $84 billion) and constitutes 40 percent of the laundry detergent market in North American. The pods were one of its most successful new products in several years and they had come to represent 70 percent of the detergent capsule market.[10] After considerable backlash, P&G changed the packaging to be opaque, added more visible warning labels, and added a third latch to the lid of the container, making it harder for children to open.

Who are other predominant advertisers?

The chart below outlines the major advertisers in the United States and around the world.

Rounding out the top twenty advertising spenders in the United States are Toyota, Johnson & Johnson, Walmart, JPMorgan Chase, Samsung, Time Warner, Pfizer, Target, Macy's, and Bank of America, each of which spent between $1.5 and $2 billion.

Worldwide, the remaining top twenty advertisers are Reckitt Benckiser (RB), Naspers, Sony, AT&T, Nissan Motor, Johnson & Johnson, PepsiCo, Pfizer, Ford Motor, and Fiat Chrysler.

There are a couple of interesting things to note when comparing U.S. to global ad spending. First, only four companies are on both lists: Procter & Gamble, General Motors, Pfizer,

---

10. Serena Ng (November 18, 2013), "Safety Experts Raise Concern over Popular Laundry Packs: New Alarm Bells over Single-Dose Detergent Capsules as Risk to Children," *Wall Street Journal*. Retrieved April 12, 2016 from http://www.wsj.com/articles/SB1000 14240527023036189045791679807304068 64.

Major Advertisers United States and Worldwide 2015

United States		Worldwide	
Procter & Gamble	($4.6 billion)	Procter & Gamble	($10.1 billion)
AT&T	($3.3 billion)	Unilever	($7.4 billion)
General Motors	($3.1 billion)	L'Oreal	($5.2 billion)
Comcast	($3.0 billion)	Coca-Cola	($3.3 billion)
Verizon Communications	($2.5 billion)	Toyota Motor Corp.	($3.2 billion)
Ford Motor Co.	($2.4 billion)	Volkswagen	($3.2 billion)
American Express Co.	($2.4 billion)	Nestle	($2.9 billion)
Fiat Chrysler	($2.3 billion)	General Motors	($2.8 billion)
L'Oreal	($2.2 billion)	Mars Inc.	($2.6 billion)
Walt Disney Co.	($2.1 billion)	McDonald's	($2.5 billion)

Source: *Ad Age Marketing Fact Pack* 2016. See also Adbrands.net.[11] U.S. spending is through July 13, 2015; worldwide spending is through December 7, 2015.

and L'Oreal. Second, Coca-Cola and McDonald's are in the worldwide top ten but do not even appear in the top twenty of U.S. spending. In the case of Coca-Cola, it's easy to see why. In the United States, several initiatives aimed at reducing childhood obesity—including one by former First Lady Michelle Obama—have targeted sugar-laden soda as a key contributor in kids' unhealthy diets and weight gain. Sales of the product have declined in recent years as people have switched to drinking more water. Much in the same way that tobacco companies increased marketing overseas after cigarette smoking dropped in the United States, so too the food companies have moved their focus to "emerging" markets. While McDonald's is not a top corporate spender, that is because it is a single entity and not a multibrand company. As we will see below, McDonald's *is* one of the top ten brand spenders. Telecommunications and

11. *Advertising Age* (December 21, 2015), "Marketing Fact Pack: 2016 Edition," pp. 8–9. See also *Adbrands*, "Worldwide Advertisers/ Agencies," at http://www.adbrands.net/top_global_advertisers. htm.

cars dominate on the U.S. list while consumer packaged goods and food companies prevail worldwide.

In the United States, cellphone carriers are constantly in a heated competitive environment. This leads to significant advertising spending, with each company trying to beat out the other with deals like paying customers to change carriers or reducing the cost of a new phone to next to zero, thus significantly reducing switching costs for customers. The battle heated up even more as telecom companies began eliminating annual contracts. In the automotive segment competition also exists, but the need to advertise comes from a different motivation. Cars are a high-end product and, unlike toothpaste or soda, are an infrequent purchase. Because there is no designated season for car buying (other than what the industry has created), there is the need to be visible to consumers whenever they come into the market to buy a car. Therefore, car manufacturers want to make sure that they are always in the prospective buyer's consideration set, which means having a continual advertising presence.

What are the most advertised brands in the United States?

The leader is AT&T, which spent $1.44 billion in 2014. Verizon, AT&T's leading competitor, is not far behind, with $1.29 billion. If you think you see the Geico gecko often, it is because you do: $1.16 billion in spending. Rounding out the top ten are McDonald's ($935 million), Chevrolet ($888 million), Walmart ($867 million), Sprint ($828 million), Macy's ($757 million), Toyota ($736 million), and Nissan ($703 million). Just as we saw from a company perspective, the most advertised brands are in the telecom and automotive segments, each with three brands in the top ten.

What is the relationship between advertising and the media?

Advertising is the primary financial support for the media that we watch and read. Magazines and newspapers have a dual revenue stream of advertising and subscriptions, but the latter has declined significantly, particularly for newspapers, as content has moved online. Basic cable television networks, too, have two main forms of income: advertising and carriage fees, money that cable operators like Spectrum or Comcast pay to have the network in their lineup. These fees can be substantial; for example, MTV's 2013 monthly average was 39 cents per subscriber and the network had 99 million subscribers, which puts their annual revenue from cable operators at close to half a billion dollars.[12] This system, too, is coming under pressure from "cord cutters" and "cord nevers," people who are canceling their cable subscriptions in favor of viewing content online or those who never subscribed to begin with. Television broadcasters—ABC, CBS, NBC, and Fox—primarily make money through the sale of advertising time on their programs.

An interesting power dynamic has arisen due to the changing fortunes of the advertising industry. In the early days of television, producers created TV shows, teamed up with an advertiser, and brought the entire package to the network looking for time on air. Shows like *Texaco Star Theater* and *Colgate Comedy Hour* were presented with a single advertiser attached. After the game show scandals of the late 1950s (where the advertisers influenced the outcome of the games) and as production costs increased starting in the 1960s, networks began selling commercials to several advertisers that appeared in "commercial pods" throughout the show, which is the system that exists today. Under this scenario, the networks began to wield considerable power because while they needed the advertising revenue, the advertisers needed access to consumers more. Remember, this was a time of mass media and a limited number of national media outlets.

12. Mara Einstein, *Black Ops Advertising: Native Ads, Content Marketing and the Covert World of the Digital Sell* (New York: OR Books, 2016), p. 23. Retrieved February 5, 2015 from http://www.trefis.com/stock/via/articles/244083/reinvention-of-mtv-will-drive-the-networks-advertising-growth/2014-06-23.

There were the three major broadcast networks and a handful of local broadcast channels in each city. There was no cable to speak of, and 90 percent or more of the audience was watching one of the three major broadcasters on any given night. Even as cable developed, the media had the upper hand versus the advertisers because most cable companies were owned by the same conglomerate that owned the broadcast networks. In the last few years, however, all of this has begun to change—in part because of the Internet, which has significantly reduced the cost of advertising, but more importantly because of social media, which have turned us into advertising distributors. Now that advertisers have an effective, less expensive option to television, the media outlets are more willing to go out of their way to attract advertising spending.

Television marketing executives developed new forms of advertising that give marketers considerable influence over the content. We saw that in the P&G "Thank You Mom" example, where the company paid for an integrated segment on *The Today Show*. Branded segments like this have become commonplace on the morning news programs because they are easily inserted into the format, the network can charge a premium fee, and the advertiser likes it because it has the feel of being an natural part of the program—that is, it works more like public relations than advertising because it doesn't look like a commercial.

A corollary to brand integration is product placement, when a client pays to have its brand appear in television shows or movies. This form of advertising became popular in the early 2000s after Mark Burnett successfully used this in *Survivor*. It wasn't by choice. CBS was in a ratings slump and when Burnett approached the network about the show, CBS executives said they would only put it on the schedule if he brought advertisers with him—just like in the early days of TV. The reality format, like the a.m. news format, works well for product integrations. On *Survivor*, people who have been starving or haven't bathed or brushed their teeth become genuinely excited about receiving Doritos or mouthwash as prizes for winning an in-show competition. That was only the beginning: products began showing up in any manner of programming from reality to contest to scripted series. We will address this again in Chapter 6 when we talk about media.

Traditionally there has been what was known as the separation between church and state—that is, between editorial (articles or TV shows) and advertising. Advertisers wanted to be integrated into the content, but they were thwarted because producers wanted to maintain the integrity of their programming. Today, because of the flight of advertising dollars to digital, producers are more open to integrating products and marketing messages if it will help persuade advertisers to spend more money. This is not only happening in fictional content but appears on news as well. Beginning in the 1980s, when companies demanded efficiencies and media companies became increasingly consolidated, news divisions were expected to be profit centers for the company—something that had not happened previously. This is because news was considered to be sacrosanct, a public good that should be outside the purview of commerce. What followed was the shuttering of expensive international news divisions and reductions in expensive investigative reporting. Instead, local news divisions began running more video news releases (VNRs), which are video versions of a press release. These puff pieces look like a typical news story but rather than unbiased reporting, they contain commentary by paid experts and beautifully shot footage paid for by the company. Online we are seeing a considerable increase in news content that is in truth advertising dressed up to look like news. This is called *native advertising*, or more broadly *stealth marketing*, and we will discuss this at length in Chapter 7.

Advertising and media have a symbiotic relationship. TV networks have long produced programming based on the need to generate the largest audience possible because the bigger the audience, the more money they made from advertising. In the early days of television, this was easy. But by the 1980s, when cable became more widely available, programming became as much about who the audience was as the size of the audience overall. A vast majority of advertisers want to reach young, affluent consumers, and we can see the effect of this on the programming produced. In the mid-1980s, upstart network Fox broadcast shows like *In Living Color* and *21 Jump Street* to appeal to this demographic, which enabled them to differentiate themselves from the traditional networks. At the same time, The WB and UPN used similar strategies with shows like *Buffy the Vampire Slayer, Charmed*, and *Dawson's Creek*.[13] Entire cable networks are devoted to attracting the attention of teens and young adults, from MTV to Freeform (formerly ABC Family). These networks create programs that will appeal to this younger audience so they can deliver the right audience to the advertiser. It has even been the case that a network will create programming to attract a specific advertiser and not just to appeal to a particular audience. In the 1990s, MTV tried desperately to get Nike to advertise on the network. Today it is hard for us to imagine this, but there was a time when sporting goods advertisers did not see a connection between sports and music. In order to attract those advertising dollars, the MTV marketing department—not the programming department—created *MTV Sports*. This was an extreme example, to be sure. What is starting to happen today, however, in terms of the influence of advertisers on content is strikingly similar. The only difference is that instead of networks determining content, advertisers now prescribe to programmers what they would like to do.

Advertising and media have become so intricately entwined that the fate of one affects consequences for the other, and the long-term impact of this is yet to be revealed. What we know for now is this: media outlets have to scramble for revenue in a

---

13. These networks subsequently folded and were replaced by My Network (owned by the Fox Entertainment Group) and the CW (jointly owned by CBS and Warner Brothers).

way they never have before, and advertisers can no longer use traditional media to reach a mass audience because large audiences simply no longer exist, with a few limited exceptions. Given this, it should not surprise us that media outlets have put aside their ethics in pursuit of profit, especially since the companies are all publicly traded entities. As for advertisers, they are moving their spending to less expensive, individually targeted communications.

How is advertising spending distributed across different media formats, such as television, print, and digital?

Television is the largest advertising medium, with $67.1 billion projected to be spent in 2016, representing 35 percent of advertising spending in the United States. Worldwide, that number is $214 billion.[14]

While television is still the leader, increasingly money is moving into digital advertising, now up to $59.7 billion. Internet advertising spending grew by more than 18 percent from 2014 to 2015 and is expected to increase another 15.6 percent in 2016, while television spending is up only 0.6 percent. Worldwide, the numbers are similar: spending is projected to be $160.2 billion, which is up 14.4 percent over 2015 spending, while the percentage increase the year before was 17.2 percent. The main recipient of those digital dollars was Google, which generated $50 billion in ad sales in 2015, followed by Facebook with $17 billion.[15]

14. *Advertising Age* (December 21, 2015), "Marketing Fact Pack: 2016 Edition," p. 15.
15. Jack O'Dwyer (January 2015), "The Year in Review," *O'Dwyer's*, p. 12. Retrieved November 21, 2016 from http://www.odwyerpr.com/magazine/odwyers-magazine-january-2015.pdf. Other media spending declined. Print saw an 11 percent decline in advertising revenue and radio dropped more than 3 percent. Ninety-nine magazines folded in 2014 versus fifty-six in 2013. Newspaper revenues are at $20 billion, down from $47 billion in 2007.

Newspaper spending is projected to be $18.5 billion, which is down 7 percent from 2015 and has been falling precipitously over the last decade because of the rise in digital and the shuttering of numerous publications, including stalwarts like the *Rocky Mountain News* and the *Seattle Post-Intelligencer*. Radio spending is flat with $17.6 billion; magazine spending is down 1.8 percent with $17.1 billion; and outdoor and cinema spending is up 4.1 percent to $9.8 billion.

Both in the United States and worldwide, advertising spending continues to grow despite the movement of money into digital.

What is the impact of digital media on advertising spending?

The Internet's share of spending has been steadily increasing over the last decade. While this medium accounted for less than 10 percent of advertising spending in 2007, today it is projected to reach 31 percent of spending. Thus far the majority of that money has been coming out of newspapers. In the United States, in 2007 newspapers represented 28.1 percent of ad spending. Today that number is 10.9 percent. Worldwide, those numbers are 26.8 percent versus 12.8 percent.

The implications of this are considerable. The economic model of the industry as we know it is imploding, and executives have seen this coming for more than a decade. We will get into more depth about this in the remainder of the book. For now, it is important to bear in mind that the advertising industry as we know it is going through a massive upheaval that will have consequences for us in terms of the quality of the content we receive and how much we will have to pay for it.

How much does advertising cost?

Ads that appear within top-rated television shows command top dollar from advertisers. *Big Bang Theory* gets $289,621 for a thirty-second commercial and *Modern Family* $236,269; *Walking Dead* and *Empire* command a whopping $502,500 and $521,794, respectively. It is even more expensive to advertise during sports programming, because sports attract a large number of men and advertisers want to reach them with their messages. One thirty-second ad in *Sunday Night Football* costs $637,330.[16]

Specialty programs, particularly shows like the *Academy Awards* that generate significant ratings, can cost four times that amount. Of course, the most expensive ads are in the *Super Bowl*, which most recently commanded $3 million for thirty seconds. Advertisers are willing to pay this steep price because of the size of the audience (more than 100 million people), who is watching (everyone—men, women, young and old), and the level of engagement (many people watch the Super Bowl just to watch the ads—something that doesn't happen with other programming).

Magazine pricing is based on circulation—that is, how many people read the publication. Unlike broadcasting, which is looking to generate a large audience, magazine publishers want to create specialized readerships that will appeal to advertisers—golfers, runners, knitters, news junkies, and so on. The more well-defined the better because the publication can charge more for the advertising. Where the ad appears in the magazine is also important. The back cover, for example, is the most expensive page in the publication because even someone who never opens the magazine may still see the ad. Popular publications charge rates that are similar to the prices charged for primetime TV commercials. *O, The Oprah Winfrey Magazine* charges $219,555 for the back cover of its publication

16. Brian Steinberg (September 29, 2015), "TV Ad Prices: Football, 'Empire,' 'Walking Dead,' 'Big Bang Theory' Top The List," *Variety.* Retrieved May 14, 2016 from http://variety.com/2015/tv/news/tv-advertising-prices-football-empire-walking-dead-big-bang-theory-1201603800/.

and *Vogue* charges $196,535 for a page inside its print publication.[17] Advertisers are willing to pay these types of fees because they want to reach a particular audience within an environment that works well with their message. Subscribers come to trust the publications they read month in and month out, which is also good for advertisers. You may also notice that advertisers will often use spreads (two-page ads) or even multipage advertising. The more advertising they buy, the bigger the discount on the per-page rate.

Radio, newspapers, and outdoor ads, such as billboards and phone kiosks, are local advertising. They are less expensive than the national TV and magazines we've just discussed because they cover a limited geographic area. The costs will also vary based on the size of the market. Advertising in New York is very expensive because it is the largest market in the country in terms of population. Advertising in Dallas would be considerably less costly.

Why is advertising so expensive?

As noted earlier, advertising revenue pays for the programming we see on television and the articles we read in newspapers and magazines. Particularly in television, it is very expensive to produce a scripted program with big-name stars. A thirty-minute television sitcom costs approximately a million dollars per episode. A one-hour drama costs approximately $3 million an episode. Series are bought as either thirteen episodes or twenty-two episodes. The major broadcasters (ABC, CBS, NBC, and Fox) have twenty-two hours (or in the case of Fox fifteen hours) of primetime to fill. Given this, you can begin to see how expensive this type of

17. "O, The Magazine Media Kit." Retrieved May 1, 2016 from http://www.omediakit.com/r5/home.asp; "Vogue Media Kit." Retrieved May 1, 2016 from http://www.condenast.com/brands/vogue/media-kit.

programming is.[18] Sports programming is even more pricey; news programming and reality series are less expensive.

Similarly magazines are expensive to produce. Articles need to be written. Photographs need to be shot. Layouts need to be created. Beyond that, the paper itself is costly, as is postage to get the publication to your home. Similar to what is happening in television, magazines are increasing their use of advertorials, print ads that look editorial, in order to lure advertisers. The only indication this content is advertising are words like "Special Advertising Section" printed across the top of the page, though these may be obscured by design elements or barely visible because of a light typeface.

On the other hand, Google produces no content, so the company can afford to charge next to nothing for advertising.

How do advertising agencies make money?

Traditionally there was a standard agreement that advertising agencies received 15 percent of the media they purchased. That is because when agencies first started they were really brokers for newspapers and not strategic and creative entities. To pay agencies for getting the business and handling collections and so on, the media would pay a 15 percent commission. So, if an ad cost $100,000, the client paid the advertising agency and the agency paid the media $85,000 while keeping $15,000 for itself. In the early days of advertising this made sense. Today, not so much—particularly because of the inflated price of TV advertising. After all, why should an agency get paid $450,000 for placing a $3 million commercial on the Super Bowl? It costs very little for them to do this. On the other hand, why would an advertising agency recommend less expensive media (like

18. Networks typically pay the producer of a TV show a licensing fee to air an episode twice. That fee covers 80 percent of the cost of producing the show. The producer must cover the rest of the cost. This is known as deficit financing. If the show is a hit, it will be sold into syndication and the producer will recoup his or her monies.

digital) when they make no money on it and it costs them a lot of money to track the advertising buy?

Ad agencies can be paid by media commission (though typically less than 15 percent), by markups on the work they do (such as creating a commercial or print ad and adding to that), or by fees or retainers, turning agencies into consultants rather than valued partners. Traditionally clients worked with an agency for years or decades, with the agency acting almost as an extension of the company. The company would be responsible for all aspects of the advertising and would be known as the agency of record, or AOR. Agencies are less likely now to be seen as trusted partners. It was estimated in the mid-1990s that one-third of advertisers still used the traditional commission system; the same number used a fee-based system; and the remainder used a combined system made up of commissions, fees, and/or incentives.[19] While there are no published recent figures, we can make an educated guess that those numbers have continued to move away from the commission-based model. When the initial shift occurred, the hope and expectation was that by removing the media commission, agencies would be more focused on strategy and creative than how much they could spend on media. What happened instead is that the AOR model is all but dead, according to *Advertising Age*.[20] Clients turn to agencies for project work and, in response, agencies offer an increasing array of fee-based services like product placement, sponsorships, and branded entertainment. Alternatively, they focus on strategy, acting more like management consultants than creative producers.

19. Andrew Jaffe, "Has Leo Burnett Come to the End of the 'Free Overservice' Era?" *Adweek*, December 6, 1993, p. 46; Melanie Wells and Laurel Wentz, "Coke Trims Commissions," *Advertising Age*, January 31, 1994, p. 2.
20. Michael Farmer (June 17, 2015), "The Death of the Agency of Record Is Near," *Advertising Age*. Retrieved April 10, 2016 from http://adage.com/article/guest-columnists/death-agency-record/299047/.

Who pays the advertising agency?

The client.

Broadly, the client is the company whose product is being sold. This could be Jeep or Butterfinger or Pepsi or Barbie or any of the thousands of products across dozens of categories that you see being promoted every day.

Within these companies there is a marketing department. If it is a large consumer packaged goods (CPG) company, each product will have a brand manager who oversees all the marketing (the 4Ps), ensuring that the product works with the placement, which works with the pricing, and so on. So, if a promotion for a free bottle of conditioner will be shrink-wrapped to a bottle of shampoo, the brand manager must work with internal operations to produce the combined product, must work with the advertising agency to develop the creative, and then must make sure the promotional version of the product is available in stores at the same time that the advertising will appear in media. The brand manager is the person the account executive at the advertising agency engages with on an ongoing basis.

In the past, it was not unusual for clients to have five-year marketing plans. Today, that is rarely the case. While not all marketing is done on the fly, the ability to "pivot" is built into corporate marketing. What does continue to have a longer-range focus is strategy—who the brand is targeting and what the brand wants to communicate to them.

Who are the major media companies that depend on advertising revenue?

There are six major media companies: Disney, Comcast, Twenty-First Century Fox, Time Warner, CBS, and Viacom.[21] It is estimated that these six companies control 90 percent of

21. For a comprehensive list of media ownership, see http://www.cjr.org/resources/index.php.

the content that we watch and read. For example, Comcast is the largest cable operator in the United States, accounting for almost a third of cable subscribers. (Comcast now has 22.3 million video customers, 23.3 million Internet customers, and 11.5 million phone customers.[22]) Comcast owns NBC and its many cable networks that include entertainment outlets like USA, Bravo, E!, and Syfy, among others, and news networks like MSNBC and CNBC. It owns Universal Studios and Universal theme parks. It was also just announced that Comcast is buying DreamWorks, makers of a number of animated movie franchises such as *Shrek, Madagascar,* and *Kung Fu Panda*. You could do this same exercise with any of the other media behemoths on this list.

These companies exist because of media consolidation that began in earnest during the 1990s.[23] Companies had started looking for financial efficiencies in the 1980s in response to Wall Street demands. Creating vertically integrated companies seemed to be the way to achieve this. Vertical integration means that the company owns multiple aspects of the production process so that it can take profits all along the way. So, for example, Universal produces *Law & Order*. The show airs on NBC and it appears in syndication on the USA Network. All of these are divisions of Comcast. Of course, they are not the only ones to do this. Twenty-First Century Fox owns 20th Century Fox and the Fox Television Network as well as numerous cable networks, including Fox News, FX, National Geographic, and local cable sports networks such as YES, the network of the

22. Jon Brodkin (February 3, 2016), "Comcast Shrugs Off Years of Cord-Cutting Losses, Adds 89K TV Customers," *Ars Technica*. Retrieved April 9, 2016 from http://arstechnica.com/business/2016/02/comcast-shrugs-off-years-of-cord-cutting-losses-adds-89k-tv-customers/.
23. B. H. Bagdikian, *The New Media Monopoly* (Boston: Beacon Press, 2004); Robert W. McChesney, *Rich Media, Poor Democracy: Communication Politics in Dubious Times* (Champaign-Urbana: University of Illinois Press, 1999).

New York Yankees. *Family Guy*, a hit show produced by 20th Century Fox, first appeared on the Fox network. This should not surprise anyone. Internally produced shows are more likely to be put on the schedule than one produced by a competitor, all things being equal. The show is sold into syndication by Twentieth Television, also owned by Fox. The show reportedly sells for $2 million an episode.

Another reason for media consolidation was the changing regulatory climate and the changing TV landscape. By the late 1980s, cable television had expanded to include dozens of popular networks that successfully competed against broadcast networks. Cable networks also have two advantages over broadcast: most receive a steady income from cable operators and many of them had begun making enough revenue that they could begin to produce their own programming. Starting in the 1970s through the early 1990s, broadcasters were not allowed to produce content that appeared on their air because of the Financial Interest and Syndication (fin-syn) rules. These regulations stated that broadcasters could not have a financial stake in programming they aired, nor could they benefit from subsequent syndication of these shows.[24] The Federal Communications Commission repealed these rules in 1993, which led to a considerable shakeup in the industry. Suddenly companies that produced programming could own a television network. Disney bought ABC because of this. At the same time, major production companies began to worry if they would have an outlet for their programming (this would turn out to be unfounded), and so Paramount launched UPN and Time Warner created The WB. Thus, the stage was set for media companies to have to be fully integrated in order to compete with one another. And now with the increasing success of online media properties, we are beginning to see traditional media companies taking

24. Mara Einstein, *Media Diversity: Economics, Ownership and the FCC* (Mahwah, NJ: Lawrence Erlbaum, 2004).

a stake in digital upstarts. NBC, for example, has invested in BuzzFeed and Vox.[25]

Looking specifically at digital corporations, here too there is considerable consolidation. Four players control the majority of the business: Apple, Amazon, Google, and Facebook. Some might also include AT&T and Verizon in this group as all of these companies, even the ones we think of as technology companies, are moving into content production. Apple has Apple TV and is producing its first original series starring Dr. Dre—the same person who got a windfall from the company when it bought his Beats headphones business.[26] Moving beyond vertical integration to horizontal integration (owning companies across industries) is Google, which has produced everything from cars to robots.

In response to media consolidation, there was a corresponding amalgamation among advertising agencies. Whole full-service agencies that had been in business for decades became subsumed within larger and larger holding companies. In other cases, agencies spun off and consolidated their media divisions in order to be able to bargain effectively for their clients. When an agency controls billions of dollars in advertising spending, the networks are more likely to pay attention.

Are media still heavily dependent on advertising?

Absolutely. Even with all the changes that have occurred in the media landscape, advertising remains the most important

25. Jeanine Poggi (August 18, 2015), "What NBCU's Investments in BuzzFeed, Vox Could Mean for Advertising," *Advertising Age*. Retrieved October 20, 2015 from http://adage.com/article/media/nbcu-s-investments-buzzfeed-vox-advertising/300005/7j.
26. Adam Epstein (February 12, 2016), "Apple is Reportedly Producing Its First Original Series, Starring Dr. Dre," *Quartz*. Retrieved April 8, 2016 from http://qz.com/616164/apple-is-reportedly-producing-its-first-original-series-starring-dr-dre/.

financial support for media. Advertising-supported networks can no longer sit on their laurels, however. There is simply too much competition, not only from other networks but also from YouTube, Facebook, Netflix, and Amazon.

How are television networks making up the advertising revenue lost to digital media?

Product placement became an increasingly popular form of marketing. Products began popping up in programming because of the introduction of Tivo, which allowed viewers to zip past commercials within recorded programs. To make sure viewers could not skip past the advertising message, products were placed within the shows themselves. Brand integration, not just placing the brand in the show but integrating it into the content, has also increased. NBC took this one step further by decreasing the number of commercial minutes appearing during some its programming in order to allow for more time for branded content. On Leap Day the network partnered with American Express to include more (Amex-branded) content during three shows, *The Voice, Blindspot,* and *Late Night with Seth Meyers,* while eliminating eighteen minutes of commercials. The network has announced they will do the same thing with *Saturday Night Live* on an ongoing basis. They will reduce the commercial load by 30 percent, which will likely increase the price of existing commercials, while charging a premium for the branded content within *SNL.*[27] If this proves successful for NBC, other networks will surely implement this strategy as well. On its face, this seems like a good thing for viewers: less commercial clutter and more programming content. But beware: the content may start looking like the early days of television, except instead of Dinah Shore singing "See the

27. Jeanine Poggi (May 2, 2016), "Live from New York: One-Third Fewer Ads!" *Advertising Age,* p. 8. Retrieved November 21, 2016 from http://adage.com/article/media/snl-air-fewer-commercials-season/303697/.

U.S.A. in your Chevrolet" we'll be watching Seth Meyers tell jokes about Doritos, or more likely we'll see him espouse how delicious they are.

As mentioned above, cable networks make money from advertising as well as from cable operators. Until recently, the broadcast networks did not receive funds from cable operators even though they deliver a larger audience than most cable networks. While it was not until the Cable Television Act of 1992 that cable operators were required to pay broadcasters for the rights to retransmit their signals, it would be another decade or more before the cable operators would actually start paying. Much of this had to do with the competitive environment; in 1992 a broadcaster who wanted to reach a large audience had to be on the local cable system. Now, however, with the increased availability of satellite TV, alternative providers like FIOS, and the Internet, broadcasters have multiple options for reaching audiences and are in a stronger negotiating position with cable operators because they can pull their signal with fewer consequences. These fees are paid for "retransmission consent" and the networks have aggressively pursued them, often to the detriment of consumers.[28] For example, when Disney was negotiating with Time Warner Cable in New York City in 2000, Time Warner didn't like the deal and pulled the ABC signal off its system. You can imagine the uproar from viewers who could not see their favorite programming. Eventually, Time Warner gave in but not before paying handsomely, not only for ABC but also ESPN, ABC Family, and a host of other Disney content.[29]

28. Broadcasters have come into new revenue because of retransmission consent, but that is beyond the scope of this discussion. For an explanation of this see: Mara Einstein (2010), "Regulating Diversity: The Effect of Retransmission Consent on the Consolidation of the Television Industry," *Free Speech Yearbook 44*, 85–94.
29. Bill Carter (May 2, 2000), "Blackout of ABC on Cable Affects Millions of Homes," *New York Times*. Retrieved May 14, 2016 from http://www.nytimes.com/2000/05/02/business/blackout-of-abc-on-cable-affects-millions-of-homes.html?pagewanted=all.

New York saw another particularly bitter fight between CBS and Time Warner in 2013.[30] Similar events between cable operators and broadcasters have occurred throughout the United States in big and small markets, and these continue today.

Media consolidation helps companies manage declines in advertising revenue. In the example just discussed, ABC negotiates all of its networks as a package with cable companies. So while the cable system may not want to carry ABC Family, it will not readily give up ESPN. By bundling the networks together, Disney helps generate more revenue for the company overall. In addition, because the companies own television production divisions, these can be money generators both in the United States as well as overseas. By producing content in house the networks can reduce acquisition costs and the content can later be sold into syndication. Moreover, the networks are all owned by companies that produce movies, a medium that does not depend on advertising. Finally, the companies have online content as well. Notable here is Hulu, a joint venture of Fox, Disney, and Comcast—and a triumvirate that would be illegal in the television environment. Look for this online streaming service to continue to get more attention from these companies as apps and subscriptions become a more dominant revenue model. CBS, which is the only one of the four major broadcasters not part of this venture, had to create its own app—CBS All Access—which at $6 a month is hardly competitive.

How is the advertising business structured?

Paralleling the media companies, there are a handful (in this case five) dominant players: WPP (London), Omnicom and the Interpublic Group (both based in New York), Publicis (Paris),

30. Brian Stelter (December 27, 2013), "TV Blackout Wars in a Quiet Period," *CNN*. Retrieved May 14, 2016 from http://money.cnn.com/2013/12/27/technology/tv-blackout-wars/.

and Dentsu (Tokyo). These are holding companies made up of a number of agency "brands" around the world and include not only advertising agencies, but also PR companies, sales promotion, and media buying, among others.[31]

WPP is the world's largest agency, with $19 billion in revenue. It is followed by Omnicom Group ($15.3 billion), Publicis Groupe ($9.6 billion), Interpublic ($7.54 billion) and Dentsu ($6 billion). Included in WPP, for example, are well-known agency names such as J. Walter Thompson (JWT), Young & Rubicam, Ogilvy & Mather, and Grey Advertising. These are connected to four major global media networks: Mindshare, Mediacom, MEC, and Maxus (known together as GroupM).[32]

As mentioned, a key reason for consolidation was the ability of the agencies to negotiate favorable rates for their clients. The companies also had better internal efficiencies because of reduced overhead. In addition, globalization of brands required that agencies be able to service their clients in multiple locations around the world and have expertise in multiple promotional platforms. This led to the joining of different types of marketing services within one company as well as the creation of multinational agency groups. Finally, the rise of integrated marketing communications (IMC) led to a decline in traditional media in favor of a broad menu of services through which clients could engage with consumers through "360-degree touchpoints."

There are three types of traditional ad agencies: the worldwide network, the "micro-networks," and independent agencies. There are approximately fourteen global networks, and they include stalwarts such as BBDO, Saatchi & Saatchi, and Leo Burnett. These companies service the big multinational companies like Coca-Cola and Unilever. All but one of them

31. Some might also include Havas in this group, though they are mid-sized in comparison to the other five.
32. To see a full list of agencies and their holdings, go to *Adbrands.net*, "Worldwide Advertisers/Agencies." Retrieved April 13, 2017 from http://www.adbrands.net/agencies_index.htm.

are part of one of the "big five" holding companies. The "micro-networks" are similar to these major global networks, except they have four or five worldwide offices as opposed to a hundred or more. These include companies like Bartle Bogle Hegarty and Wieden & Kennedy. The smaller agencies have reputations for being particularly creative, so they may develop the strategy and the creative and then the work will be distributed by one of the larger networks. Independent agencies are smaller and more specialized. Upstart agency Droga5 is a good example here. This award-winning agency is known for producing cutting-edge creative for companies like Chase, Under Armour, Android, and Diet Coke. Independents have been receiving more attention of late because clients see them as being more creative and more nimble in terms of trying new media options.

A word here about consolidation within media agencies. In the simplest of terms, the media arm of an agency is responsible for planning what media to use and then negotiating with the individual media vehicles (TV network, print magazine) to get the best price and placement for its ads. Most large agencies have spun off their media departments as separate global businesses. We saw this with the example of WPP. In terms of buying, this arrangement enabled WPP to achieve economies of scale because it was buying for several clients at once. As for planning, the intention is to encourage "media neutrality," whereby the agency will look for the best media to suit the campaign rather than what will make the agency the most money (i.e., television). This sector, too, is dominated by global networks, such as Mindshare, Carat, or Starcom MediaVest.

How much time do we spend with media and why does that matter?

Advertisers want us to spend as much time as possible with media so that they can get their messages in front of us. Gradually we are spending more and more time with media content, and that number should take off significantly as more content moves to mobile. Think about it: in the past our media interactions were limited to a couple of hours a day of television, some time listening to the radio on the way to and from work, and perhaps the newspaper in the morning and a scan of a favorite magazine at night. Today barely a moment goes by when we are not connected to some mode of communication that is pushing advertising on us. In the past we would have gotten onto an elevator and been quiet with our thoughts or engaged in conversation with others around us. Not anymore. Now as soon as the door shuts, we pull out our mobile device and start checking our emails, Facebook, or BuzzFeed—all of which have their accompanying advertising. Or maybe you read the *New York Times* or search for something on Google. You'll find ads on those sites, too. While we may think of our phone as a communications tool, it is first and foremost a purveyor of advertising.

On average, Americans spend twelve hours and five minutes per day with media. Until very recently, most of that time was spent with television, which occupies approximately four hours of our day and has done so for decades. While that seems like a lot of time, when you break it down the numbers add up. If you watch a half-hour in the morning while getting dressed, maybe another half-hour before dinner, and then three hours of primetime, that's the four hours. Of course, there may be more viewing on the weekend. In 2013, our time spent with digital first overtook TV viewing (4:48 versus 4:31). By 2017, it is projected that we will be spending close to six hours a day with digital media (5:56) and less than four with television (3:58). Digital continues apace because the technology has been designed to keep us connected. Mobile devices are like pacifiers, never leaving our sides. Our addiction to these devices is fueled by notifications that send pings of reward cues to the brain. One study showed that social media were more addictive than smoking, drinking, spending money, sleeping, and sex. Still other statistics demonstrate how tethered we've become: office workers check their email thirty to forty times per hour; we move between devices twenty-one times per hour and Facebook users are on the site eighty-one hours per year. Americans spend almost three hours per day on tablets, and two hours per day using smartphones for things other than voice.

Digital is made up of desktop or laptop devices, mobile, and other connected devices (this can include gaming consoles, for example). By 2014, mobile had already overtaken desktop as the leading digital method for transmitting advertising. This trend will continue as advertisers are becoming smarter about how to track us through our mobile devices and how best to serve ads to us there. Technology is also allowing advertisers to be able to track us across devices as well as intermarry data across our online and offline activities. And don't forget multitasking. Most people use a secondary device like a cellphone or a tablet while watching TV. We may be tweeting along with a favorite show or looking up how to buy an outfit we saw on air. Whether television or radio, cellphones or tablets, these technologies exist for the distribution of advertising—first to last.

3

CONSUMER BEHAVIOR

What is consumer behavior?

Consumer behavior is defined as "the mental and emotional processes and the physical activities of people who purchase and use goods and services to satisfy particular needs and wants."[1] Let's break this down a bit. "Mental and emotional processes" means that consumer behavior—how we buy, what we buy, when we buy, and how we dispose of a product—is based on how we think and feel about it. Thoughts and feelings about a product can be manipulated through marketing techniques; that's the whole point of this business function and it is the premise behind branding. Physical activities are the various ways that people spend their time in relationship to the market, including how we buy products; how we talk about products; and now, because of social media, when, why, and how we share product information. Understanding who people are emotionally, psychologically, and physically enables marketers to use the 4Ps to create products and promote them in ways that will most resonate with the consumer, meaning you and me. Finally, the ultimate goal here is to "satisfy needs and wants" through the purchase of

---

1. William O. Bearden, Thomas N. Ingram, and Raymond W. LaForge, *Marketing Principles and Perspectives*, 2nd ed. (Boston: Irwin/McGraw-Hill, 1997), p. 99.

consumer goods and services. The idea that the market is the best mechanism through which to fulfill our individual needs and wants is a fundamental tenet of late capitalism and neoliberalism. This is also the basis for much advertising criticism due to three key reasons: 1) it turns happiness/fulfillment into a goal (and now happiness itself is widely marketed) rather than more socially responsible or ethical pursuits, 2) achieving this happiness is based on individual wants and needs rather than what is good for communities or the wider society, and 3) many wants, and even some needs, have been artificially produced by advertisers.

When did advertising become based in psychology?

During the age of mass media (read: TV) and mass marketing in the 1950s and 1960s, there were two competing schools of thought: one promoted a rational sell (known as the head sell or the hard sell) and the other an emotional sell (the heart, or soft, sell).

The hard sell was based on the Unique Selling Proposition (USP), a concept devised by Rosser Reeves of the Ted Bates agency. A USP defined products by a unique attribute and then proceeded to hammer that message into consumers' minds over and over *and over* again. M&M's "melts in your mouth, not in your hand" is a good example, as is Geico's "Fifteen minutes can save you 15 percent or more on car insurance." The rational sell assumes that there is something new to say and that products have significant differences they can promote. Marketers call this "new news." A hard sell works well for large companies like P&G and Unilever that spend significant sums on research and development in order to garner new ideas and products. This approach also works well when consumers are in the market for a product that will serve a specific purpose. What medicine is best for cough and flu? What car gets more gas mileage? And so on. Most products have some level of a rational sales component and some products will continue to be best sold using this message strategy. I'm thinking here of laundry detergents that tell you how clean your clothes can get or Walmart that tells you about its low, low prices. Far more prevalent is the soft sell, which means using emotions to induce consumer interest and attention. This method was advanced by David Ogilvy as well as Leo Burnett, both of whom were influenced by motivation research, which suggested that archetypal images would unconsciously attract consumers to brands. Pulling consumers to the brand through image and emotion is at the heart of the soft sell.[2] As we saw, Ogilvy did this with Dove and other brands. Leo Burnett became known for creating characters in conjunction with its clients' products—the Jolly Green Giant for Green Giant vegetables, Charlie the Tuna for Starkist, and the Marlboro Man. Tying the product to a person helps to evoke emotion. People relate to people (even animated ones) more than they can relate to a cigarette or a can of tuna. We see this idea continue today with characters like the Geico Gekko and Flo for Progressive Insurance as well as in corporate CEOs who are almost indistinguishable from the brands, like Steve Jobs and Apple. In social media, CEOs or celebrities or Vine stars or someone with lots of Facebook friends or Twitter followers are influencers, individuals who sell the brand to others. Online this is crucial because the sales pitch is one-to-one, not mass marketing. Expect to see an increasing number of "spokescreatures," animated characters like Charlie the Tuna. They provide marketers with the ability to embed their message in a character (something they cannot do with a celebrity) while maintaining control of the brand narrative.

The emotional sell gained traction through the 1960s and into the 1970s during the time of the creative revolution on

2. D.B. Holt (2002), "Why Do Brands Cause Trouble? A Dialectical Theory of Consumer Culture and Branding," *Journal of Consumer Research* 29(1): 70–90.

Madison Avenue. The baby boomer population was more highly educated than previous generations, and the industry responded with more sophisticated messages using urbane humor and emotional images and promoting lifestyle benefits rather than the frankly dumbed-down ideas of the USP. Behavioral psychologists became integral to industry practices. "Advertising agencies started to talk about 'end end benefits' as opposed to just 'end benefits,' meaning the final consumer satisfaction in emotional terms rather than the physical satisfaction to be gained on the way there," according to Saatchi & Saatchi executives Pringle and Thompson.[3] In order to learn what emotional benefits were most relevant to consumers, it became of paramount importance to understand who the consumers are, what concerns them most, and what will fulfill their lifestyle aspirations. McDonald's "You deserve a break today" ads from the 1970s is a good example here. Instead of touting their fries or the value of their food or even specifically telling Mom she didn't need to cook, the commercial highlights that McDonald's is a place to get away from the everyday, almost as if it was a vacation destination. With a catchy jingle sung over images of a happy family going to the restaurant are the words "You deserve a break today. So get up and get away to McDonald's." The agency used this emotional appeal because it resonated with women who were increasingly in the workplace, and finding themselves juggling jobs and kids and home. They weren't thinking about giving their kids a healthy meal or looking to get something on the go. They told the agency in focus groups that they saw McDonald's as "a break."

Evolving communications theories were also instrumental in moving advertising toward a psychological sell. Older communications theories worked under the idea that whatever message was sent to a mass audience was received

3. H. Pringle and M. Thompson. *Brand Spirit: How Cause Marketing Builds Brands* (New York: John Wiley, 1999), p. 72.

and understood verbatim by everyone in the same way. The Hypodermic Needle Theory, for example, suggested that communications worked like giving the audience a vaccination—shoot them up with the content and they will accept whatever's placed in front of them. We think this is silly now, but the idea had developed as a model to explain the success of Hitler's propaganda tactics. By the 1970s that notion had been put to rest. Rather, new communication frameworks posited that a message (TV show, movie, or advertisement) is encoded by a source, the message is sent through a communication channel, and then it is decoded on the other end by the receiver of the message. The receiver—that is, the audience—may or may not interpret the message in the same way it was encoded. This makes more sense as a working theory. The audience is not a homogeneous, indistinguishable mass, and who we are and what our life experience has been affect how we respond to advertising messages, movies, or a TV show. Knowing this, it became incumbent upon advertisers to learn who their consumers were and what drove them, not only from a demographic perspective but from a psychological one.

How do advertisers discover these consumer insights?

Have you ever watched a commercial and had thoughts like "How does Prudential know I haven't saved enough for retirement?" or "How do Nike and Under Armour understand that I like to picture myself as an Olympic sprinter when I'm running (even if I know it will never happen)?" or "Boy, Purina really gets that Oliver the cat is a family member." The advertising connects so completely with your thoughts of yourself or your emotional state that you get almost an eerie feeling that the advertiser has been peering in your window.

Well, advertisers have not been doing that, but they have been accumulating a tremendous amount of research to understand how we think about and interact with their products. Research begins with examining what is understood about consumers through existing data, known as secondary research. Secondary research is information from outside sources, and it is helpful in getting a broad overview of what is going on in a product category. For example, a major supplier of consumer data is Nielsen, the same company that does the TV ratings. When you go to a supermarket or drugstore and your purchases are scanned, that information—scanner data—is picked up by Nielsen. Advertisers can use this information to see who their competitors are as well as which are the most popular brands in a category. So, for example, Coca-Cola would see that sales are declining. The brand manager would then look to see if people are drinking competitors' products instead, or if they are turning to alternatives, such as water, tea, or juices. Other companies that generate large-scale consumer research are Simmons and GfK MRI. These companies have been surveying American consumers for decades about product and media usage, all of which can be analyzed across demographic groups. If a company wanted to find out who eats frozen pizzas and what kind of television programming they watch, these surveys would provide those answers. It would also tell them which brands were most popular across different genders and age groups. Secondary data is a starting point to determine the target audience and to decide if there are niche targets, to identify sales trends as well as cultural trends, and to assess the competition. Information based on surveys that generate numerical outcomes is called *quantitative data*.

In addition to companies like Simmons and Nielsen that examine consumers broadly, many research companies specialize in topics such as social trends or in understanding important demographic groups that advertisers want to know about. Trend Watching (trendwatching.com) looks at consumer insights from around the world. A recent report, called *The Future of Betterment*, looks at the trends shaping health and wellness. Standing desks have become the rage, diet fads come and go, and meditation apps have become almost as ubiquitous as music apps. In and of itself, this is all noise. The underlying insight is that people are concerned about health and fitness in a way that has not been true before. Driving this trend is a push toward self-actualization, an idealized version of self that sits atop Abraham Maslow's hierarchy of needs. Says Trend Watching, "In 2016, *consumerism* is the primary means by which people pursue that search [for self-actualization]. The brands they'll notice, engage with, love, are those that *help them be the people they want to be.*"[4] The very idea of this is horrifying and confirms this as a main point of criticism as discussed at the beginning of the chapter. However, marketers take this to heart and use it as a means to sell health and wellness to us. For example, one aspect Trend Watching notes is that while we want to be healthy, actually sticking to a healthy lifestyle is quite difficult—less than 3 percent of Americans fulfill minimum requirements for doing so. Marketers, therefore, are told to build healthy aspects into the environment, to create ambient health opportunities, so that health can occur with little effort on the part of the consumer. Starbucks teamed up with Philips to create "EnergyUp cafes" in the Netherlands where lamps that mimic natural daylight are placed in the stores. These lamps improve mood and revitalize customers after twenty minutes. Think about that; you go into Starbucks and feel better after having spent time there because of a sun lamp. Either way, you are likely to go back to the store because you want to experience that good feeling again. In another example Headspace, a meditation app company, is working with an architectural firm to create Headspace Meditation Pods to be placed in airports, schools, and parks. Waiting for a plane, why not use the time to meditate? And if you do it with your Headspace app, all the better.

Millennials are a demographic group of particular interest to advertisers, and several companies specialize in this

4. *Trendwatching* (April 2016), "The Future of Betterment." Retrieved April 30, 2016 from http://trendwatching.com/trends/the-future-of-betterment/.

generational cohort. The Cassandra Report has for twenty years provided marketers with insights into the millennial generation. One insight, for example, is that they are socially conscious and expect companies to demonstrate this in their brands. Thus, TOMS Shoes and Warby Parker are popular with these consumers because of their socially responsible corporate ethos to give away shoes or eyeglasses with each pair purchased. The report has now expanded to cover the emerging Gen Z, those born between 1998 and 2008 (demographic cohorts are covered in more detail below). While these are children aged 8 to 17, they have considerable influence on household purchases and therefore are of interest to marketers. Another company that focuses on millennials is Ypulse, an aggregator of research as well as a producer of demographic studies. This company provides ongoing insights into what appeals to young adults, from fast food to Coachella to the emerging trend of the return of the vinyl record. From their own studies, they have looked at social media usage among this group and found that "only 2% say they don't use any social platform," and they spend "11 hours and 26 minutes with smartphones daily" mostly messaging or using social media.[5] Insights like these direct marketers' thinking about what products to develop, what images to put into advertising, and what media to use to convey their messages.

These are just a few examples of the many places where marketers can find secondary data.[6] Secondary research can also be found in academic journals, particularly the *Journal of Consumer Research*, the *Journal of Marketing*, or the *Journal of Advertising*, which contain work done by marketing professors from top business schools. Census data is an important

5. Ypulse (April 26, 2016), "5 Stats On Millennials, Teens & Social Media." Retrieved April 26, 2016 from www.ypulse.com/post/view/5-stats-on-millennials-teens-social-media.
6. Others widely used sources include The Pew Research Center (http://www.pewresearch.org/), Forrester, and eMarketer. See appendix for additional resources.

source for information about changing population trends. Increasingly, consulting companies are providing research white papers as a way to induce business-to-business customers. They promote these items for free as a lead generator so that they can capture emails from prospective customers.

Secondary data, particularly research from the larger companies, tends to be quantitatively based. This information is helpful for understanding broad trends and competitive information. However, in order to get more in-depth understanding about consumers, particularly consumers of individual products, marketers need to use qualitative research methods.

Qualitative research is information that cannot be quantified by numbers. You can ask people in a survey how many times a week they use a product. It is much more difficult to ask them why they picked Ben & Jerry's over Häagen-Dazs. For those sorts of insights, companies will use focus groups. These are groups of ten to twelve people who are in the demographic range of the marketer. The group is led by a moderator who asks a series of questions that have been determined based on what the client and the account team need to know. Maybe there is another kind of ice cream that consumers have begun to discover, or the group voices concerns about health and calorie counts, or maybe they don't like the company's politics. The focus group is all about sussing out these types of insights. In addition to product information, focus groups are used to test advertising concepts before a commercial is produced. Participants are shown a concept statement and asked what it means to them, or they might be shown a rough version of what a commercial might look like using existing footage and a voiceover. Then they will be asked what the message conveyed. Based on the group's responses, the final commercial can be tweaked accordingly. In-depth interviews are another form of quantitative research. These interviews can be several hours in length and are used for research into topics that are not easily discussed within a group, death and life insurance being a good example. Finally, marketers can also use observational research. This entails monitoring consumers within a specific environment, perhaps a mall or a restaurant. The most extreme form of this type of research is ethnographic studies, which entail observing consumers within their "natural habitat," which is usually their home but could be at parties or the gym. Ethnographic studies differ from observational studies in that the researchers interact with the subjects. Researchers from the kids' channel Nickelodeon have been known to move in with subjects to find out what they really buy and what media they really watch as opposed to what they say they buy and watch. A growing number of research companies specialize in marketing ethnography. These firms are able to generate rich insights into consumer behavior, such as why people select one vodka over another when purchasing for the home versus in a bar or what hinders people in motivating themselves to work out.[7] These studies are not limited to the real world. Researchers also execute these studies online, which is known as netnography.

How do we decide what to buy?

When determining what it is we want to buy, we go through the consumer decision-making process. This entails five steps: need recognition, information gathering, evaluation of alternatives, purchase, and post-purchase behavior. Need recognition is realizing that our current state of being is not what we would like it to be. The need might be as simple as "I feel hungry" or it might be "I need a new computer because my old one is taking twenty minutes to load up." Once we recognize

7. Graeme Wood (2013), "Anthropology Inc.," *The Atlantic*. Retrieved March 20, 2013 from http://www.theatlantic.com/magazine/archive/2013/03/anthropology-inc/309218/; Herzong Naurach (August 24, 2013), "The Adidas Method. A German Firm's Unusual Approach to Designing its Products," *The Economist*. Retrieved February 10, 2015 from http://www.economist.com/news/business/21584002-german-firms-unusual-approach-designing-its-products-adidas-method.

this need, we can go about fulfilling it. Note here that this may be a true need (I'm hungry) or a want generated by advertising (I've got to have the latest Frappuccino or Xbox or lipstick from Sephora). Next, we begin to look for information about products that might create equilibrium. If we are hungry, we don't need this information-gathering step, but if we are buying a computer, we most certainly do. A snack is a low-involvement product, while a computer is a high-involvement product that requires more attention and consideration. We might look online to see reviews of possible computers, or go to a Best Buy or the Apple store and try out a few models, or ask friends about their computers. We might even look at advertising. Once we have exhausted the information search, we evaluate alternatives. Do I want something salty to eat or something sweet? Do I need a laptop or a desktop? In the latter case, am I willing to give up computing power for portability? After sorting out the options, we make our purchase. But it doesn't end there. The last step, and what some would argue has now become the most important, is post-purchase behavior. That is, what is the company going to do to keep you as a loyal customer and what are you going to do in terms of your purchase? While in the past this might have entailed getting people to sign up for a warranty, today the goal is to get people to go online and talk about the product on social media. Online sites like Facebook, Twitter, and Instagram have been increasingly important in the information-gathering step of this process, and the more people get recommendations from their friends about a product, the more likely they are to believe it is a worthy product. Today, moving from need recognition to purchase can take place in moments and all in the palm of your hand. This has been facilitated by companies being able to interact with you at multiple "touch points" throughout the process.

Parallel to the consumer's decision making is the marketer's sales funnel, which consists of awareness (alerting customers to a product, often through advertising), consideration (similar to evaluation of alternatives), preference (deciding for one product over another), and action (purchase). Traditionally, the only place advertisers would be able to influence purchase decisions was at the point of awareness, and if someone was shopping in a store, preferences could be influenced by a salesperson. With online shopping, marketers can constantly put sales messages in front of us. You've probably experienced this when you put a pair of jeans into an online shopping cart and then, after you decided you didn't really need them, the jeans started following you from your computer to your phone to your iPad. Because of the ability to interact with us at multiple points throughout the decision-making process, the path to buying has become more of a spiral than a straight line. So, for example, we might be ready to buy a computer, but then we see a friend post on Facebook that she loves her new Microsoft Surface, which sends us back to the information-gathering stage and evaluating still more alternatives.

What influences our purchase choices?

Social and psychological factors affect the products we buy. Social factors may be personal factors, such as family and culture, which are demographic characteristics, or nonpersonal influences, such as time, place, or environment. Psychological factors are tied to emotions and cultural factors that are connected to psychographic characteristics.

What are demographics?

Demographics (or "demos") are statistical information about who we are such as age, income, ethnicity, education level, and gender. How old we are, what kind of work we do, our education level, our religious background, and how many children we have all factor into purchase decisions. If you work in advertising, you dress as if every day is casual Friday; on Wall Street, suits are the norm. If you have kids, backpacks, snack

packs, and school supplies are on your list. And, if you aren't
Jewish, you may not have ever tried (or bought) gefilte fish.
Cultural factors come into play here as well. Some basic
tenets of being an American, for example, are the idea of the
pursuit of happiness, abiding individualism, and the American
Dream. In addition, we all belong to subcultures, which might
relate to religion or life stages or areas of interest. College students are a subculture that purchases backpacks and electronics; surfers buy board shorts and sunscreen; country-western
fans buy ten-gallon hats and cowboy boots. These subcultures
are what sociologists call our reference groups, and they influence our buying behavior.

What are some of the key demographic cohorts?

Generational groups have similar lifetime experiences and
advertisers tap into these shared experiences in an attempt to
relate a product with their target audience. Generation cohorts
active today are baby boomers, Generation X, millennials (also
called Gen Y and Echo Boomers), and Gen Z.

Baby boomers are people who were born between 1946 and
1964. Just after World War II, the birth rate skyrocketed: by
the time it started to taper off in 1964, there were more than
seventy-four million boomers representing 40 percent of the
population.[8] As this generation grew, so did the move to the
suburbs. Soldiers returning after the war were supported
by the G.I. Bill, which gave them access to free college and

8. Researchers put different timeframes on these generational cohorts,
   so reports disagree about which generation is biggest. All agree
   that Generation X is the smallest group, and millennials are becoming the largest population group, while boomers are declining.
   Some sources are claiming that Gen Z is the largest group; not yet,
   but this is likely to be the case within a few years. These numbers
   are from the *U.S. Census* (June 25, 2015), "Millennials Outnumber
   Baby Boomers and Are Far More Diverse, Census Bureau Reports."
   Retrieved May 2, 2016 from https://www.census.gov/newsroom/
   press-releases/2015/cb15-113.html.

funding for mortgages so that living in a house was suddenly less expensive than residing in an apartment. They grew up in a time of political and social unrest. Civil rights, the women's movement, and the Vietnam War defined this generation, as does the fact that they are more educated than previous generations.

Baby boomers were the first generation to be defined as a consumer generation. They grew up with Barbie dolls and Disney's Mouseketeers, and Frisbees. They continue to be avid consumers in their fifties and sixties, but they are also still defined by their experiences. Many still see themselves as activists fighting for social change; they don't like to think of themselves as aging even while they are entering into retirement. You can see this idea in many commercials targeting this age group. Financial services and healthcare are the top categories for this group, so we see commercials for Cialis that show active couples still interested in participating in regular sexual activity, or Depends ads showing Lisa Rinna, star of *Days of Our Lives* and *Melrose Place*, looking utterly glamorous and sporting these undergarments as if they were Spanx and not adult diapers. Importantly, they do not like to think of themselves as having aged. Hallmark cards made the mistake of creating a special line of cards for baby boomers. It failed miserably because boomers didn't want to look for cards "in the old people's section." Their attention is on their children and grandchildren and staying active and healthy to enjoy their time with them. While advertisers have tended to stay away from consumers over the age of fifty, today they are beginning to notice that this group has considerable disposable income—70 percent of it, in fact. Baby boomers have an estimated spending power of $3 trillion. Many of their favorite brands are tied to their youthful roots and ideas of individualism and breaking free from the establishment. These include brands such as Levi's, Volkswagen, and Harley Davidson. They also like brands they established relationships with in the 1960s and 1970s, such as Frye boots, Absolut vodka, and

Clairol hair color.[9] Areas where they tend to spend are related to health and financial services, but they outspend other demos in coffee, diet sodas, and magazines; they lead in technology adoption; and because they have time on their hands, they are the biggest consumers of media.[10]

Generation X is defined as those born between 1965 and 1981. They are the sandwich generation—not as interesting as the boomers and past the age when advertisers are interested in them. Also, this group is smaller (66 million) than boomers (74.9 million) and millennials (75.4 million), who in the last year have now surpassed boomers in size.[11] Unlike the cohorts that surround them, there are not many ways in which this group is particularly distinct, whether we are talking about politics, religious values, ethnic makeup, or economic circumstances. Cultural icons that defined this generation are MTV, AIDS, *The Simpsons*, "Space Invaders," and *The Breakfast Club*. They do tend to be more conservative (Republican) and more economically pessimistic. This is, perhaps, justified. They are the generation of the "McJob." They hit their prime earning years at the time of September 11th, which was quickly followed by the Great Recession, and many got caught in the housing bubble, buying properties when they were at the height of the market and then ending up underwater when values crashed. They grew up during a time of increasing divorce rates and many

9. CNBC (n.d.). "Favorite Brands of the Boomer Generation." Retrieved May 15, 2016 from http://www.cnbc.com/2010/03/01/Favorite-Brands-of-the-Boomer-Generation.html?slide=10.

10. *Huffington Post* (n.a.) (August 17, 2012), "Boomers Are 'The Most Valuable Generation' For Marketers, Nielsen Report Finds." Retrieved May 3, 2016 from http://www.huffingtonpost.com/2012/08/17/marketing-to-boomers-most-valuable-generation_n_1791361.html.

11. Richard Fry (April 25, 2016), "Millennials Overtake Baby Boomers as America's Largest Generation," *Pew Research Center.* Retrieved May 3, 2016 from http://www.pewresearch.org/fact-tank/2016/04/25/millennials-overtake-baby-boomers./

were "latchkey kids," which may account for their tendency to be very family oriented.[12]

As a group they have been ignored by marketers. Boomers have more disposable income. Millennials are establishing buying habits and pride themselves on being influencers. While Gen Xers are making more money than millennials, as a group they are not as important to understand, if for no other reason than simply because of their size. There are a few product categories, however, that buck this trend. Movies that harken back to their youth are a great example. Films like *Pitch Perfect* that use the current musical trends of group singing insert generationally targeted songs and movies (*Breakfast Club!*) into the film's plotline. Amazon grew its business by focusing on the core values of Gen Xers. This generation is tech savvy, pessimistic, and incredibly busy. Amazon created a site that tapped into their tech capabilities, gave them lots of information to help assuage their pessimistic tendencies, and made shopping easy, reliable, and less expensive.[13]

Millennials are those born between the early 1980s and the early 2000s.[14] As a group they are disconnected from politics and religion, connected via social media, overloaded with debt, and distrustful of people, and they are postponing marriage,

---

12. Jon D. Miller (Fall 2011), "Active, Balanced, and Happy," *The Generation X Report*. Retrieved May 3, 2016 from http://home.isr. umich.edu/files/2011/10/GenX_Report_Fall2011.pdf.
13. Paul Taylor and George Gao (June 5, 2014), "Generation X: America's Neglected 'Middle Child'," Pew Research Center. Retrieved May 3, 2016 from http://www.pewresearch.org/fact-tank/2014/06/05/generation-x-americas-neglected-middle-child/ ; *McDonald Marketing* (2012), "Gen X Marketing Guide." Retrieved May 15, 2016 from https://www.independentagent.com/Resources/ StaffDevelopment/Diversity/SiteAssets/DiversityTrainingSeries/ training-series-materials/Gen-X%20Marketing%20Guide.pdf.
14. There is disagreement about what dates to use to define this generation. I've seen it described as 1977–1994. Most typical, however, is early 1980s to early 2000s. No matter which way the dates are selected, however, this demographic is large and growing.

according to the Pew Research Center.[15] They have been widely characterized as having a prolonged adolescence, leading to feelings of entitlement, self-centered behavior, and digital addiction. An MTV study noted that their principal concerns are getting a job, graduating college, and moving out of their parents' house: not much different from previous generations. Where they diverge, however, is that they are "later to launch"— that is, they are inclined to put off adulthood (and marriage) for as long as possible. Some of this was fueled by helicopter parenting, wherein they were special, everyone got an award for sporting events whether they won or lost, and rarely did they hear the word "no."[16] Societally, they grew up in a time of abundance. Yet that world was shattered by September 11th and economic recessions in 2000 and 2008. These are the "digital natives," who only know a world with on-demand technology, and they fluidly move through their online and offline lives.[17]

15. *Pew Research Center* (March 7, 2014), "Millennials in Adulthood: Detached from Institutions, Networked with Friends." Retrieved September 13, 2015 from http://www.pewsocialtrends.org/files/2014/03/2014-03-07_generations-report-version-for-web.pdf.

16. Mary Burns (September 26, 2013), "The Millennial Generation at Work," lecture presented at the Kellogg Alumni Career & Professional Development.

17. There is an ongoing academic debate about whether digital technologies are improving social relations or making us more atomized and disconnected. Those believing in the positive aspects of this include Lee Rainie and Barry Wellman, *Networked: The New Social Operating System* (Cambridge, MA: MIT Press, 2012); danah boyd, *It's Complicated: The Social Lives of Networked Teens* (New Haven, CT: Yale University Press, 2014); and H. Jenkins, S. Ford, and J. Green, *Spreadable Media: Creating Value and Meaning in a Networked Culture* (New York: New York University Press, 2013). Less sanguine about this are Clay Sharky, *Here Comes Everybody: The Power of Organizing Without Organizations* (New York: Penguin, 2008); Astra Taylor, *The People's Platform: Taking Back Power and Culture in the Digital Age* (New York: Metropolitan, 2014); Robert McChesney, *Digital Disconnect: How Capitalism Is Turning the Internet Against Democracy* (New York: The New Press, 2013); and Siva

Advertisers are interested in this group for a number of important reasons.[18] First, they are young and have not established brand loyalties with many product categories. Associated with finding new brands is that the members of this generation are at the time of their lives where they are moving away from home and starting their own families—even if they are doing it at an age that is older than their parents were. This life cycle stage is one in which people tend to spend more money. They are getting married, having children, and buying or renting homes. Moving to a new address generates considerably more spending over the first six months than established homeowners spend in two years, with money being spent on furniture, cleaning supplies, and neighborhood services such as banks, hair salons, and restaurants.[19] Second, millennials account for 24 percent of the US population, making them the biggest generational cohort.[20] Finally, they are a generation immersed in brand culture, readily interacting with brands, talking about them, and recommending them to friends both online and off.[21] Selfies, FOMO (fear of missing

Vaidhyanathan, *The Googlization of Everything (And Why We Should Worry)* (Berkeley: University of California Press, 2011).

18. Micah Solomon (December 24, 2014), "2015 is the Year of the Millennial Customer: 5 Key Traits These 80 Million Consumers Share," *Forbes*. Retrieved March 11, 2015 from http://www.forbes.com/sites/micahsolomon/2014/12/29/5-traits-that-define-the-80-million-millennial-customers-coming-your-way/; Jeff Fromm, Celeste Lindell, and Lainie Decker (2011), "American Millennials: Deciphering the Enigma Generation." Retrieved March 11, 2015 from https://barkley.s3.amazonaws.com/barkleyus/AmericanMillennials.pdf.

19. *Experian Marketing Services* (n.d.), "Life-Event Triggers." Retrieved September 13, 2015 from http://www.experian.com/marketing-services/life-event-marketing.html.

20. U.S. Census data.

21. *MarketingCharts Staff* (September 16, 2014), "Millennials Mostly Talk About Brands Offline. Which Media Drive Their W-O-M Impressions?" Retrieved March 25, 2015 from http://www.marketingcharts.com/traditional/millennials-mostly-talk-about-brands-offline-which-media-drive-their-w-o-m-impressions-46011/.

out), and crowdsourcing drive the members of this group, who pride themselves on knowing about the latest product and being able to tell others about it. Millennials are more likely than boomers to share brand preferences via social media (57 percent versus 31 percent) and they are more likely to claim that "people seek me for knowledge and brand opinion" (52 percent versus 35 percent).[22] A stunning 81 percent recommend brands to people by word of mouth, according to MTV, and 74 percent believe they influence the purchase decisions of their peers, according to research from Intel.[23] And, they influence not only each other but also other generations. Baby boomers have embraced Facebook in no small part to connect with their millennial offspring; the same is true of Instagram, texting, and pretty soon Snapchat.

Members of Generation Z, the newest cohort, are beginning to garner considerable attention from advertisers. Just as marketers keyed in on millennials at a young age, this group is no different. Part of this had to do with marketers targeting younger and younger audiences. Having tapped out existing consumers, in the search for new markets advertisers look to different age groups, and kids had been an untapped market. Over the last few decades we have seen kids' marketing explode from toys to movies to food to makeup (the last two having negative consequences such as childhood obesity and possible hormonal risks from using makeup).

Even so, marketers want to tap into this market because these youths significantly influence household purchases. One study found that these tweens and teens have at least some say

22. Christine Barton, Lara Koslow, and Christine Beauchamp (January 15, 2014), "How Millennials Are Changing the Face of Marketing Forever," *BCG Perspectives*. Retrieved March 25, 2015 from https://www.bcgperspectives.com/content/articles/marketing_center_consumer_customer_insight_how_millennials_changing_marketing_forever/.
23. Ypulse Conference (June 17, 2013), presentation by Berj Kazanjian, SVP Ad Sales, Consumer Insights, and Research, MTV; Sandra Lopez, Marketing Strategy Director for New Business, Intel.

in 93 percent of family purchases.[24] This can be anything from cars to computers to food choices and family vacations. It can also be media selection, a reason why movies that appeal to kids and families have done so well at the box office; Marvel films and *The Lego Movie* are good examples. Members of Gen Z also have their own money to spend—an average of $16.90 per week, which translates into $44 billion in the aggregate.[25]

Simply because of their age and lack of experience, they are going to differ from other age groups. However, since millennials were previously studied, marketers are able to make generational comparisons. Notably, feelings about money and politics are very different for this group because they were raised during the Great Recession and they have never known a world without the "war on terror." This likely accounts for the members of Gen Z being more focused on money, with 60 percent (versus 44 percent of millennials) claiming that having a lot of money is a measure of success. They have traditional ideas of ownership in terms of homes and cars, which may not bode well for the "sharing economy" in the long term. They have bought into the entrepreneurial ideology: 62 percent want to start their own companies rather than working for an established enterprise. To that end, they have begun (already!) to build their skill set, including using their free time to develop general business skills (58 percent) as well as tech-based skills, such as graphic design (51 percent), shooting and editing videos (50 percent), and creating apps (50 percent).[26]

24. *EY* (2015), "What If the Next Big Disruptor Isn't a What But A Who?" Retrieved May 10, 2016 from http://www.ey.com/Publication/vwLUAssets/EY-rise-of-gen-znew-challenge-for-retailers/$FILE/EY-rise-of-gen-znew-challenge-for-retailers.pdf.
25. Sylvan Lane (August 20, 2014), "Beyond Millennials: How to Reach Generation Z," *Mashable.* Retrieved May 2, 2016 from http://mashable.com/2014/08/20/generation-z-marketing/#1Z8n3ZQTSPqQ.
26. *Deep Focus* (March 30, 2015), "Deep Focus' Cassandra Report: Gen Z Uncovers Massive Attitude Shifts Toward Money, Work and Communication Preferences." Retrieved May 2, 2016 from http://www.marketwired.com/press-release/deep-focus-cassandra-report-gen-z-uncovers-massive-attitude-shifts-toward-money-work-2004889.htm.

This factors into this group being the ultimate multitaskers, having truly grown up as digital natives. Research shows they use five screens to millennials' two.[27] They communicate more with visuals than verbiage and their attention span is limited. Note, however, that current research suggests that attention spans are at eight seconds for all groups, which is less than that of a goldfish. Two other defining factors are that this group is truly multicultural and accepting of a variety of lifestyle choices, and they are protective of their privacy and prefer secrecy in their communications (Snapchat and Whisper versus Facebook).

This generation's practicality translates into what they expect from brands. They are pragmatic, so they want narratives with realistic endings (67 percent). This search for the "real" means that members of Gen Z are big fans of YouTube, which they use more than any other type of social media (85 percent), and they prefer brands to communicate with them through this platform.[28] For now, there are no "Gen Z brands" other than the technologies they engage with.

Are women more important to advertisers than men?

Overall, yes.

Women are a more important demographic group because they account for $4.3 trillion (72 percent) of US spending. Globally, that number jumps to $20 trillion. Women still do the majority of household shopping, but they also decide on purchases such as home furnishings (94 percent), vacations (92 percent), cars (60 percent), and consumer electronics

27. *Sparks and Honey* (June 17, 2014), "Meet Generation Z: Forget Everything You Learned About Millennials." Retrieved May 2, 2016 from http://www.slideshare.net/sparksandhoney/generation-z-final-june-17/56.
28. *Deep Focus,* Cassandra Report.

(51 percent).[29] Women account for 78 percent of consumer purchases.[30] Creators and advertisers of individual products, however, are only interested in reaching their particular target audience. So while women are an extremely important group and the focus of the vast majority of advertising (which makes the study of advertising and consumerism a feminist issue), for some brands like Budweiser or Axe men will be more important.

What are psychographics?

Psychographics divide consumers into groups based on their personality, values, and lifestyle rather than their age, income, and gender. The earliest framing in this way was called VALS, which segments adults into eight types based on motivations and resources, which are important determinants of what a person will choose to buy. For example, high-resourced "Achievers" are goal-oriented (achievement motivated), committed to their job and family, and particularly conscious of their peers. "Makers" (low resources and motivated by self-expression) distrust government, like the outdoors, and believe in defined gender roles. "Innovators" are people who always like to be in the know, like to experiment by trying new things, are skeptical of advertising, but have faith in science and research and development (R&D).[31]

29. Michael J. Silverstein and Kate Sayre (September 2009), "The Female Economy," *Harvard Business Review*. Retrieved May 4, 2016 from https://hbr.org/2009/09/the-female-economy.
30. Carl Bialik (April 22, 2011), "Do Women Really Control 80% of Household Spending?" *Wall Street Journal*. Retrieved May 3, 2016 from http://blogs.wsj.com/numbers/do-women-really-control-80-of-household-spending-1054/.
31. *Strategic Business Insights* (n.d.), "US Framework and VALS™ Types." Retrieved May 3, 2016 from http://www.strategicbusinessinsights.com/vals/ustypes.shtml.

You might be familiar with the term "early adopters." This term is usually applied to the adoption of technologies, and this group is in many ways similar to Innovators. Early adopters have to have the latest gadget or gizmo before anyone else. They like to feel like they are on the cutting edge and enjoy telling others about what they know because it feeds their sense of self as being the "go-to" person. "Alpha Moms" are a specific example of an early adopter group. According to *USA Today*, these women are "educated, tech-savvy, Type A moms with a common goal: mommy excellence. She is a multitasker. She is kidcentric. She is hands-on. She may or may not work outside the home, but at home, she views motherhood as a job that can be mastered with diligent research."[32] So, an Alpha Mom might be a young millennial mom/part-time student, or a career-driven, late-in-life Gen Y mom: different demographic profiles with similar psychological motivations to purchase. Marketers tap into these moms' self-perception of being on the cutting edge, even if it only has to do with what organic foods are best or which tutor can really help their kid. Nintendo launched its Wii gaming system by promoting the product as an exercise tool and a means to bring the family together. Nintendo recruited Alpha Moms for parties and let them try the system before it was released to the public. This promotion was so successful that the Wii outsold Sony's Playstation—the industry leader—by close to 50 percent.[33] Nintendo used psychographics to launch its product while feeding its prospective consumers' motivation to be trendsetters. More important for Nintendo is that the company took advantage of the fact that Alpha Moms would want to tell others about the product. This is known as word-of-mouth (WOM) marketing. It is the most

32. Bruce Horovitz (March 27, 2007), "Alpha Moms Leap to Top of Trendsetters; Multitasking, Tech-Savvy Women Are Expected To Be Next To Watch," *USA Today*, 1B.
33. Effie Award Entry: "Wii Want to Play" (Gold Award Winner). Retrieved February 7, 2009 from http://s3.amazonaws.com/effie_assets/2008/2331/2008_2331_pdf_1.pdf.

effective marketing there is because people trust their friends and family more than they trust advertisers. In this case, it was particularly effective because it is reported that if Alpha Moms endorse a product, they tell ten people; if they don't, they tell three hundred.[34]

This is just one example of a psychographic group. There are many, and they can be created as primary or secondary data. Nielsen, the same research company that tracks TV, online ratings, and scanner data, has sixty-six different consumer groups based on lifestyles and purchase behavior. For example, "Money & Brains" is a psychographic group defined as people who are wealthy, urban, and aged 45 to 64 and may or may not have kids in the home. More tellingly in terms of describing who they are is the information that they shop at Banana Republic, travel for business, read the *New York Times*, and drive a Mercedes E-Class. Alternatively, "Old Milltowns" is a downscale group defined as mostly retired people of various ethnicities over the age of fifty-five. They order from JC Penney, belong to a veterans' club, read *Hunting*, watch the *Judge Joe Brown* show, and drive a Ford Focus.[35] Brand companies can evaluate these psychographic groups and determine which ones are most likely to relate to their product, and then they can target their message accordingly.

Bear in mind, too, that any large group can be broken down in this way. Millennials, for example, are not homogeneous even though the media talk about them as if they are. Millennial marketer Ypulse divided this generational group into five groups. Muted Millennials live at home and are risk-averse; Supremes are high social achievers, they are the best-educated of the groups, and the majority of them are influenced by word

34. "The Powers of the Alpha Mom." May 17, 2007. *CBS News.* Retrieved June 5, 2016 from http://www.cbsnews.com/video/watch/?id=2821119n.
35. To see a full list of psychographic profiles, go to Nielsen. *MyBestSegments.* https://segmentationsolutions.nielsen.com/mybestsegments/Default.jsp?ID=0&menuOption=home&pageName=Home.

of mouth; the Moralistic Middle group have old-fashioned values and shy away from thrills; Alt Idealists are cause-oriented and highly value individuality; and Beta Dogs are very passionate, like to network, are most open to advertising, and are driven by appearance.[36] Supremes and Beta Dogs are the influencers, the people whom others turn to online for ideas about products and trends.

Why do advertisers break up the population into groups?

Advertisers are not interested in getting their message in front of everyone. They want to interact with specific groups of people whom they have determined through research to be most interested in their product, and they want to develop the "right message" for this group. This is the target audience that we discussed in the first chapter.

Marketers break up the population into groups, which is known as segmentation. One way of doing that is by demographics. As we saw, our age, gender, and occupation affect our product purchases. With psychographics, marketers tap into our values, beliefs, and lifestyles. Other ways marketers break us up into segments are by behavioral characteristics and geography. Do you live in a hot or cold climate? Is it urban or rural? Economically depressed or well-to-do? These are geographic issues affecting purchase behavior.

Behavioral characteristics take into consideration a number of factors. Is this a product that is a regular purchase or only for special occasions? Are you a heavy or light user of the product? (The rule of thumb is that 20 percent of users are responsible for 80 percent of product purchases, so this information is particularly important.) Where are you on the sales funnel—are you ready to buy or still just getting to know the product? Are you a non-user, an ex-user, a prospect, or a

---

36. Ypulse Conference (June 17, 2013), presentation by Ali Driesman, Director of Insights & Inspiration at Ypulse.

regular user? Other factors are benefit sought (convenience or prestige), loyalty status, and marketing sensitivity (price versus quality, for example).

If we look more closely at user status, we can see how this has an impact on message strategy. Current users do not need a lot of explanation about a product, so reminder advertising such as a billboard or an online banner ad might be all that is needed. For prospects, however, advertising is a bit more convoluted. As I say to my students, the most expensive customer is a new customer. Here's why. If the product is in an existing category, the objective becomes to persuade that prospect to select your brand. Fair enough. For people who already use a competitor's product, the advertiser has to provide an incentive, such as a coupon or a free sample, to get them to switch. Unless the product is significantly superior, this strategy will have mixed results since without the incentive the product is no longer appealing. Non-users need to be convinced of not only the superiority of your brand but also the value of using the product to begin with.

Know, too, that companies use either an aggregation strategy or a segmentation strategy. An aggregation strategy addresses the market with the same message, expecting that it will appeal equally across segments. This type of strategy is used with products like ice cream or Life Savers or other low-involvement products. The Gap has also used this strategy in its campaigns using celebrities and their children to appeal to multiple generations of consumers. This is atypical. Most brands utilize a segmentation strategy where they divide the population into groups and select one or more of them to be their target audience. The examples I have been using throughout the book do this, whether we are talking about Red Bull targeting millennials or Dove targeting women or cereals targeting kids and their moms. Know, too, that target audiences can change over time. When the iPod was introduced, Apple wanted to reach early adopters and in particular young people in order to project an image of hipness. Once the product became more mainstream, the advertising changed to show all kinds of people using the device. After all, baby boomers with money to spend could buy the product not only for themselves, but for their grandchildren. Thus the company moved from a very defined target audience to an aggregation strategy.

Is that why media are designed for different audiences?

Exactly. Advertisers want to reach certain groups of people. Media outlets need to attract advertising. Thus, cable TV networks and magazines are designed to attract the audiences that advertisers most want to reach.

What are target audiences?

The target audience is, quite simply, the people advertisers want to reach. This starts with gender. Is the company targeting men or women or both? Next is age: is the product right for adults or kids or everybody? From there, this can become more finely tuned based on an increasing number of demographic factors as well as psychographics and product usage. After they have segmented the market, they look at which segment or segments are appropriate for their brand.

In some cases, the target audience can be very similar. Axe is for men, and because of its overpowering scent, it tends to appeal to young men. Old Spice is also a male-oriented product, but the campaign "The Man You Want Your Man to Be" is targeted to women (though the ads are clever enough to appeal to men as well).

Other products can have different appeals to different people, all of which might be presented in a single advertisement. The iPad is a perfect example of this. In their commercials, Apple shows lots of different people using the product for lots of different activities. Teens might use the iPad to take pictures of watermelons being thrown from a building, and moms use the device to read with their children or find a recipe, and grandparents use it to FaceTime with their progeny or to share pictures of their grandchildren so they can brag with other grandparents. Teens and moms and grandparents are different market segments, but as a group they make up (at least some of) the target audience for iPads. Knowing the target audience helps with not only creating the advertising, but selecting the media through which to reach them. For example, you won't find men reading *Glamour*, and paying for *Sports Illustrated* to reach women would be wasting a client's money.

Don't get confused, however. Marketers are interested in their targets and are not so concerned about what other groups might think. For example, I don't relate at all to Mountain Dew advertising, and for PepsiCo, the parent company, that's just fine. On the other hand, Banana Republic wants my business and so they promote messages of classical style and business-appropriate clothing. But don't ask my Gen Z daughter about BR. She wouldn't be caught dead in that store.

Do marketers only want to reach buyers?

No. Marketers are interested in buyers, users, prospective users, and product influencers. These are important distinctions because the buyer of the product may or may not be the user. While you pick up Grape-Nuts or granola for yourself, children can't. In this case, an advertiser might choose to target the mother or child or both. In targeting the mother, the emphasis is likely to be on the nutritional value of the cereal. Kids could care less about that, so marketers talk about taste or a toy surprise when targeting them with hopes they will nag their mother to go shopping. It is most difficult to appeal to both. This is why the "Mikey" Life cereals are still held up as one of the great ads of all time. It got kids to pay attention while letting moms know it was a nutritional cereal that kids would actually eat.

As we see in this example, kids can be influencers on household purchases, but they are not the only ones. While men typically purchase the family car, moms are significant influencers if there are children in the home. A recent ad demonstrates this without actually showing the mother in the advertising. The commercial starts with a garage door being opened to reveal an Infiniti QX60. The man behind the wheel is expensively dressed and obviously upscale. As the car pulls out of the driveway, we see the dashboard with high-end features, and the man opens the moon roof and then tugs at the cuff of his sleeve as he moves his head in time with the music. We begin to hear the lyrics of the song that has been playing: "I'm the baddest man alive." The car comes to a halt, the man switches off the music, and a group of young girls climb into the back seat as he asks, "How was the pool?" Then an announcer comes on to say, "Built for families. Designed for drivers." The commercial communicates that the car is good for families (which mothers want) but has all the technology and performance of a high-end car (which fathers want). Another example people might remember is the Michelin tire ads that showed babies sitting on a pile of tires. This, too, was obviously meant to grab the attention of mothers, who in turn would suggest these tires to their husbands.

There are five consumer buying roles:

User: This is self-explanatory. A user is the consumer of the product, whether it is toothpaste or a download from iTunes.

Influencers: Anyone who can affect the purchase decision.

Buyers: The person who purchases the product.

Initiators: The person who recognizes the need and begins to find a solution to the unmet need.

Deciders: Whoever has the ultimate say-so when it comes to buying a product.

We can quickly see that the role someone plays in the buying decision affects how a marketer will need to address that person. If someone is all of these roles in one, that makes things a bit easier. A woman buys apparel for herself, a teen buys his or her own soda or salty snack, and so forth. Determining how best to talk to consumers becomes more complex when there are multiple players in the mix. The buyer and user may or may not be the same person. Moms buy toys for kids. Men buy flowers for Mother's Day. Children influence a myriad of household purchases, women influence decisions on cars and healthcare, and so on. Children's cereal often uses a dual target of moms (buyers) and kids (influencers) and this can be covered in the same ad. However, if the product is a bicycle helmet, the message to the mother would be one of safety and for kids it is going to be the "cool factor," so different message strategies will have to be applied. College selection is particularly complex—the user is the student, there are multiple influencers, and the final decider could be the student or the parents, who will end up with the bill. Given these roles, the marketer must determine not only whom to focus on but what role the consumer plays and if multiple players should be targeted.

What is the ultimate goal of prying into our personal lives?

Remember, advertisers want to get the right message to the right person at the right time and place—so that person will ultimately go out and buy the product. Understanding who consumers are enables advertisers to craft a message that gets their attention. In order to insert the message in the correct media so that the target will see it, the marketer has to understand who the consumer is. This was more important when advertising was primarily bought in legacy media dependent on demographics defined by Nielsen—women 18 to 49, men 18 to 25, or kids 2 to 11, for example. Today, with online media, targeting using these demos takes a back seat to one-on-one marketing.

Psychographics had been the norm for marketers, and while it is still being used, that is changing because of the vast amounts of data available about consumers through online tracking. Because of digital media and big data, companies now retain upwards of 1500 data points on every American.[37] This does not mean that research will go away. Far from it! What it does mean is that research will be more fine-tuned and more individually directed, raising serious concerns about surveillance and privacy.

37. Katy Bachman (March 25, 2014), "Confessions of a Data Broker," *Adweek*. Retrieved August 18, 2015 from http://www.adweek.com/news/technology/confessions-data-broker-156437.

4

CREATIVE

What constitutes good advertising?

The best advertising combines creativity that engages consumers and stimulates them to buy while incorporating the strategic objectives of the marketer. Balancing these two goals is at the heart of numerous battles between advertisers and their agencies: the work may be funny and creative, but it also has to be strategically on message. If not, then it is art, not advertising.

What are some examples of good advertising?

Advertising that works well brings together memorable visuals or copy or both that neatly connect the strategic message with the product. The Energizer bunny "keeps going and going." The pink, drum-playing rabbit not only cruised through his own commercials but appears to pass through commercials for other products. People want to know their batteries will last a long time, and this was an entertaining way to show this. Like today, decades ago cats doing crazy things got viewers to pay attention. Cats appearing to sing "meow, meow, meow, meow" for Meow Mix cat food told cat owners that their finicky cat would love this food so much that "they ask for it by name." Other famous copy lines include Dunkin' Donuts' "time to make the donuts," showing that their donuts were made fresh daily, and Wendy's

"Where's the Beef?" ad, which used comedy to show viewers that Wendy's burgers were bigger and better than the competition. And in a print example, we might think of "Got Milk?" and the various celebrities, from Britney Spears to Serena and Venus Williams to Bart Simpson, sporting a milk mustache. While these campaigns are decades old and no longer in use, they became part of popular culture and are still remembered today.

There is no set formula for coming up with these concepts and copy lines, but there is a process. We will look at this process throughout this chapter and see how it has been applied to come up with current advertising campaigns.

Is there a best commercial of all time?

Many consider Apple's "1984" to be the best commercial of all time. In the commercial, we see skinheads bathed in a bluish light all staring blankly at a screen where a man is droning on about ideology; it is a scene out of George Orwell's book *1984*. The only person in color is a woman in a white t-shirt and bright red shorts. She is running toward the screen carrying a sledgehammer. Behind her are menacing Stormtroopers, determined to stop her. Before they can reach her, she throws the sledgehammer at the screen, destroying it. We see a flash of white light. We see the new Macintosh computer and copy begins to scroll on top of it. The copy reads: "On January 24th Apple Computer will introduce Macintosh. And you'll see why 1984 won't be like *1984*."

This commercial communicates visually what Apple was all about without talking about the specifics of the product. IBM—known as Big Blue—was going to be destroyed by Apple, a company that doesn't follow the crowd. People who stay with the status quo are drones who don't think for themselves. Given what we know about baby boomers and Gen Xers, this was a very powerful message.

From a production perspective, the commercial has very high-end production values. The spot was directed by Ridley

Scott, famous for having directed *Blade Runner* and *Alien*, among many others. The commercial was shot to look like a feature film rather than a standard commercial. There is a huge cast, something rarely seen in a commercial. These unexpected elements are used to grab the attention of the audience, who were not used to this level of artistry. And grab attention it did: while the commercial aired only once, it received tens of millions of dollars in free advertising, appearing on news shows all over the country. What ultimately makes this commercial so effective is that it seamlessly marries the communication of Apple's breaking the model with visually arresting artistry.

What is the process for deconstructing an ad so I can analyze it myself?

First, view the ad like you normally would. After it's over, ask yourself what your initial impressions are: is it a good ad? A bad ad? Why? Did it grab your attention? If so, what about the commercial drew you in? Was it the visuals, the music, or perhaps it was your favorite celebrity? Was there something in the commercial that was offputting? If it did not appeal to you, can you think of anyone who might find the spot entertaining or informative?

Next, watch it again, but start to analyze it a bit more critically. What I like to have my students do is describe the ad aloud and in as much minute detail as they can. Keep asking yourself, "what did I see?" "what did I hear?" and "what else?" This will lead you to more specific details, such as who is in the advertising—men or women, young or old? Are they rich or poor? How do you know this? Perhaps it is the clothing they are wearing or the restaurant where they are having dinner. Describe the people in the ad and where they are situated in more and more detail. Are parents in the background while children are in the front of the screen? What does this tell you about the product and whom the advertiser is targeting?

Also think about who is *not* in the commercial. In doing this you might start to see how certain groups are not represented, such as older people, gays and lesbians, and people of color. Remember, some targets are more important to advertisers than others. The more you do this, the more you might begin to feel like the world is overrun with upscale millennials.

After assessing what you see, start to evaluate the production of the piece. Is there a voiceover? Is it male or female? What is the person saying, and how is he or she saying it? Is the voice sultry and alluring or shouting and commanding? What is the point of view of the camera—does it put you in the midst of the action or are you a voyeur? Is the camera angle shot from above or below? Is it meant to look like a shaky, amateurish production or something out of a Hollywood movie? Are there colors overlaid on the spot, such as blue on the "1984" ad, and what is that supposed to convey? Finally, how and how often is the product seen in the commercial? Who interacts with the product? Does the product act like the "hero" of the commercial—that is, does the product "save the day" by making your clothes cleaner or making your breath fresher?

Having done this work, you should be able to tell whom the product is targeting. Based on your analysis as well as your initial impressions, you should also have a good sense of what emotions the advertising is intended to evoke. Definitely you should be able to understand the key communication that the commercial is conveying.

Finally, if you opt to perform a full critical analysis, you would begin to ask yourself questions about the assumptions the advertising is making, the embedded ideologies, and these assumptions and ideas communicate to the viewer. These can be grouped in terms of gender, race, and class stereotypes. Even with the women's movement in the 1960s, we still see women predominantly appearing as mothers and wives in commercials. Even more annoying more recently is the increased use of stay-at-home dads in commercials. This has been a trend since the recession of 2008 when more men lost jobs and women became the primary breadwinners. Ads that target millennials, like Coca-Cola spots, use multiethnic casts, but ads for financial services show well-to-do older white people and ads for low-cost phones for the elderly show mixed-race casts. This, of course, subtly conveys the notion that white people not only have more money but were smart enough to save for their retirement.

Let's deconstruct a current and very obvious ad for Barbie so you can see how this plays out. Mattel has sold Barbie dolls for more than fifty years, and the company has been the number-one toy marketer because of the success of this toy. Only recently has Mattel fallen out of the top position, and that is because of the overwhelming success of *The Lego Movie*.

In an attempt to update the brand, Mattel repositioned Barbie by tapping into the concept of girls' empowerment. The commercial begins with college students filing into a lecture hall. Copy appears in a loose, handwritten typeface saying, "What happens when girls are free to imagine they can be anything?" A girl walks into the front of the room and she says she is the professor and will be teaching a class on the brain. Next we see a girl being a veterinarian. Then we see a tour guide in a museum providing information about dinosaurs (this girl is African American as a tip of the hat to diversity). Yet another girl is a soccer coach who tells the male soccer players to lift their knees higher, higher (I'm not making this up: she says to lift their knees higher "like unicorns"). Last, there is a "businesswoman" talking on her phone in an airport.[1]

All sounds good, right? Wrong. In scene after scene, the adults the girls interact with smile and giggle at them because they are obviously just so cute. But think about it. What does that communicate? If we see a girl in front of a classroom and she says she is the professor and will be teaching about the brain, and then all the students smile and laugh, what we learn

---

1. You can see the full ad here: http://www.barbie.com/en-us/youcan-beanything/.

is that girls are adorable but no one actually believes they are capable of doing what they say. This happens in scene after scene after scene in this almost two-minute commercial. It is the same pat on the head women have endured for decades while trying to break into male-dominated professions. And if you don't think this still happens, ask any woman working in a tech field what her experience has been.

In the next chapter we will examine more advertising examples and the messages they convey for individuals and society.

What are the three elements of advertising?

There are three elements of the creative process: strategy, creative, and execution. The *strategy* entails the audience the advertiser is targeting and what the advertiser wants to communicate to them. The *creative* is the "big idea" that sells the product: singing cats or Nike's "Just Do It" or Verizon's "Can You Hear Me Now? Good." *Execution* is how the commercial is put together based on the creative that has been developed. Different directors will have a different vision about how the commercial should be created. A good way to think about this is how Tim Burton might direct an ad versus how Steven Spielberg would.

How does a company decide on a competitive strategy?

Advertising exists to solve a business problem. Marketers must analyze the business environment to understand what the problem or opportunity is. Then, based on that information, they need to set objectives and develop a strategy that helps them achieve those objectives.

Companies often use a SWOT (Strengths, Weaknesses, Opportunities, and Threats) analysis in order to have a full understanding of the business environment. This tool is laid out as four quadrants with strengths and weaknesses on the top and opportunities and threats on the bottom. The top two relate to internal aspects of the company while the others provide insights into external factors. In the Nike example, a strength might be the company's longstanding relationships with athletes while a weakness might be the brand's lingering reputation as the user of overseas sweatshops. An opportunity might be to provide more coaching in their app products; a threat would be Under Armour's lead in acquiring popular fitness apps. After assessing the company and its competitors in this way, the next step is to determine the marketing plan.

Creating a marketing campaign is like going to war. Companies use a combination of objectives, strategies, and tactics to win at the sales game. An objective is the aim of the advertising: increasing sales, reminding consumers to buy the product, changing perceptions, and so on. A strategy is how the objective is going to be achieved. It is based on the information derived from research done on the category and the brand. It includes the target, the positioning, and how the company will employ the marketing mix. Tactics are the specific tools used to implement the strategy. Say a small local health club needs to compete with a national chain nearby. The objective in this case is to increase memberships, which is broadly about increasing sales. Multiple strategies could be employed. One strategy could be to try to get more people working out. Another could be to steal members from the competition. Using this latter example, a good tactic would be to put an advertisement on the bus stop in front of the competitor's door. Similarly, T-Mobile wanted to increase its user base. The strategy was to steal from the competition (and, really, that would be the only thing to do, since who doesn't have a cellphone?). They offered to pay switching charges and provided an app on Facebook so that people could send a "Dear John" letter to their former cellphone carrier.

An important factor in deciding on a strategy is the company's standing in the market. For example, a company that is the leader in the category could try to get more people to use a product overall. By growing the category, the company will increase sales by default. This is what Nike does: Nike develops its creative to say that everyone is an athlete. The company motivates more people to work out, and by default more people will buy Nike. So Nike's strategy has been about the athlete in all of us. But a company can do this only if it is the leader in the category. All the other companies either need to develop their own positioning—as Under Armour did—or they can compete against the leader. The strategic communication can be "we're better than Nike" or "we're as good as Nike, only cheaper," for example. Alternatively, the company might argue it is better than the leader, thus encouraging consumers to try its products or try them again. This was the thinking behind the famous Pepsi Challenge, where Pepsi did blind taste tests against industry leader Coke and found that most people preferred the taste of Pepsi.

How does targeting get translated into creative executions?

Whom a brand is targeting affects how advertisers communicate with consumers. After all, you wouldn't talk to your mother the same way you talk with your friends. This affects not only what advertisers say, but also how they say it.

Let's take a campaign that targets teen girls. In 2014, Always created a video called "#LikeaGirl." In this three-minute film, women and girls are asked by a director sitting next to the camera to "run like a girl" or "fight like a girl." The women responded with stereotypical depictions of what they have been asked to do. Next, adolescent girls were asked the same things. However, for them, running like a girl was simply running, and so was fighting. After seeing the girls, the director asked the adults if they would prefer to change their interpretations, and they sheepishly did. In the middle of the video, it says on screen "Always wants to change that," meaning the company wants to change the negative connotations around "like a girl." In terms of targeting for age and gender, this was very straightforward. Always, like most feminine hygiene products, wants to reach adolescent girls when they are first making decisions about what brand they will use. Knowing a bit more about what girls go through at this point in their lives provides direction for the communication. According to the brand, "Girls experience the biggest drop in confidence during puberty, around the same time as their first period. As a society, we contribute to that drop, often without even recognizing it. Always wanted to change this, so they created a rallying cry to reverse the meaning of a common playground insult to champion girls' confidence through the #LikeAGirl campaign."[2]

Another product that has an obvious target market is beer. The audience for this product is men and the age range is typically 21 to 30. While the target may be limited in this way, it will still appeal to those outside that narrowly defined range because the rule of thumb is that young people "aspire" older (teen guys want to be like their older siblings) and guys in their 30s and 40s still want to think of themselves as being in their 20s, particularly when they are sitting around watching a ballgame. The vast majority of beer ads fit this bill: "Whassup" from Budweiser, the Silver Bullet from Coors, the cutting-edge grunge of Pabst Blue Ribbon. Some brands step outside this limited frame. Dos Equis' "Most Interesting Man in the World" campaign featured a debonair man who looks to be in his 60s doing everything from parachuting to providing advice on speed dating. Beer companies have also been accused of targeting underage drinkers with commercials like Budweiser's frog ads, where three frogs on lily pads intone, or rather croak, "Bud-wei-ser." In all of these spots, the underlying communication is that drinking is fun, and it is more fun with friends.

A good example of psychographic targeting is Chipotle's "Back to the Start." As you likely know, Chipotle is a Mexican

2. Effie Awards (2015), Youth Marketing—Teens & Young Adults/North America. Retrieved May 15, 2016 from https://www.effie.org/case_studies/by_category/106.

food restaurant that promotes its organic roots. On its website, Chipotle readily promotes the local farmers it supports; indeed, the restaurant has been known to drop products from the menu at times if an ingredient cannot be sustainably sourced. The company has a passionate, loyal consumer base, many of whom stuck with the chain even after federal prosecutors began a multistate inquiry into complaints about food safety and the commensurate food-borne illnesses. That support is for the food, yes, but it is also for the ethos that the company evokes, which is based on the triple bottom line of people, the planet, and profits, and not profits alone. "Back to the Start" was a two-minute-plus animated film that aired during the 2012 Grammy Awards show. This was an appropriate venue for the ad because the program attracts a wide audience, many of whom are young and socially conscious. In addition, the spot was more like a music video than a commercial, so it would blend into the content. It featured the Coldplay song "The Scientist," sung by Willie Nelson. The visuals were an animation of a farmer realizing that he can no longer be part of a huge industrialized farm, so instead he converts his farm into a humane farm with sustainable practices, like the supplier farms used by Chipotle. As an added twist, the company directed viewers to download the song, with proceeds going to the Chipotle Cultivate Foundation. The company did a follow-up video, "Scarecrow," which included an interactive online game, and subsequently created a four-part series on Hulu called "Farmed and Dangerous." All of these appeal to the consumer target through their lifestyle sensibilities around sustainability.

What is positioning?

Positioning refers to how marketers want their target audience to think about their product, or how the product is positioned in the minds of consumers vis-à-vis other products in the category. To establish that position, marketers work to create a defined identity, something that differentiates them from the competition.

There are a number of ways to do this. One way is to distinguish the brand based on its product attributes (i.e., defining features important to the target). Microsoft's Surface uses this strategy by drawing attention to a pen that comes with the computer tablet that enables artists to draw directly on the product's surface (thus the name). This advertising employs an additional strategy: positioning against a product competitor. As Apple has long been associated with the artistic community, this ad is directly situating itself against this industry leader. Another ad that did this effectively was a 2011 Super Bowl ad called "Empower the People" that introduced the Motorola tablet, Xoom. In the commercial, people were all dressed in the same white hooded outfits and had white earbuds hanging down from their ears. The only thing of color in the ad is the guy using the advertised product. This commercial was a twist on Apple's "1984" Super Bowl ad described above. While Xoom was not ultimately successful as a product, the promotion got people's attention.

Another common method is to position the product based on who the user is. The problem with this strategy is that the field can get overwhelmingly crowded, particularly if the users are millennials. How do you stand out in that marketplace? Not easily. The top 100 brands with this generational group are the leading brands in the world. Topping the list is Apple, followed by Nike, Samsung, Sony, Microsoft, Target, Amazon, Google, Walmart, and Coca-Cola. Most of these seem pretty obvious, except for Target.[3] What this company did in terms of positioning is helpful in explaining this concept. Target has been around since 1962 and was originally a discount retailer like Kmart or Walmart. Two decades ago,

3. Mallory Schlossberg and Ashley Lutz (November 14, 2015). "The Top 100 Brands for Millennials." *Business Insider*. Retrieved May 5, 2016 from http://www.businessinsider.com/top-100-millennial-brands-2015-5.

Target repositioned itself under the concept of "cheap chic" and everything the company does feeds off that idea. Target has had limited deals with top designers (like Isaac Mizrahi, Missoni, and Marimekko) to create affordable versions of these designer brands. These partnerships have been incredibly successful for Target, in terms of sales as well as communicating the idea of top design at affordable prices. In addition, Target has added more grocery items to its store offerings so that older millennials can do one-stop shopping. And to attract younger millennials simultaneously, Target has positioned itself as the back-to-school retailer for college students. Choosing this time period was strategically purposeful: back-to-school is now the second largest selling season of the year, after Christmas.

One final positioning strategy we will discuss is positioning based on price and quality. A good way to demonstrate this is by using a perceptual map. Like the SWOT, this tool divides the market into quadrants. Those quadrants are labeled based on axes that go from low to high. Low to high what? Well, that depends on the most important factors that go into buying a particular product. For this example, we will look at the car category, with the axes being price and quality. That is because people make this purchase decision based on how much money they are willing to spend and then, based on that, they attempt to get the highest quality. Given this, the map would be divided into high price/high quality, high price/low quality, low price/high quality, and low price/low quality. For high price and quality, you would have BMW, Lexus, Infiniti, and Mercedes. For low price and quality, you would have Kia and Smart cars. Thus you can see that people in the market for a Beemer are not even going to think of a Smart car. Laying out the products on a map like this helps marketers see where their product is positioned in the mind of consumers vis-à-vis the competition. Not every perceptual map will be based on price and quality. The market can be mapped based on other factors, such as users (male/female, young/old) or product attributes (high calorie versus low calorie).

Who is responsible for creating advertising?

Advertising is created by teams of two made up of a copywriter and an art director. Based on a strategy statement or creative platform, they will generate a number of creative concepts. These concepts must then pass through the gauntlet of the creative director (who oversees all campaigns within an account), the account team, and finally the client. Along the way, the concept may be shown to a focus group of prospective consumers.

How do marketers decide what to put in an ad?

Using a combination of market research (what is going on in the business environment) and marketing research (everything the company has learned about the target consumer), advertisers will develop a message that they hope will resonate with their target audience. This information is synthesized into a short document called a *creative brief*. The information in this document is what the creative team uses to come up with the advertising.

What exactly is contained in a creative brief?

A creative brief, sometimes called a *creative platform* or a *strategy statement*, provides a distillation of consumer research and defines the elements that need to be included in the advertising for the creative team. There are variations in the format, but it will always include an objective, a definition of the target audience, a detailed product description and how consumers relate to the product, a one-line promise or consumer benefit, an accompanying one- or two-line support statement, and either a description of the brand personality or a definition of what the tone and manner should be—that is, should the commercial be serious, funny, or irreverent. Other elements that may be included are competition and known problems that inhibit usage. Bottom line: the creative platform defines who the advertising is talking to and what the advertising should make consumers think, feel, or do after having seen it.

How these elements are executed is up to the creative team—these are the creative and execution elements noted earlier.

Can you give some creative case studies demonstrating the path from problem to execution?

Let's go back to the #LikeAGirl example.

The Brief: Always needed to attract new consumers entering the market. The company faced significant competition in attracting millennial girls because other brands were doing a better job in reaching them through social media.

The brand has a decades-long commitment to empowering girls by providing puberty education. Young consumers entering the market were not familiar with the brand's purpose. Much of this was attributed to the fact that the brand was using a product attribute strategy, a major misstep as competitors were touting personal benefits, particularly through social media.

Girls first engage with Always during puberty, a time of insecurity and awkwardness. To go back to their roots of championing girls, the brand struck on the idea of putting a fresh spin on confidence.

The brief to the agency said "to create a campaign that leveraged the brand's legacy of supporting girls as they make the transition from puberty to young women, while reinforcing why the brand is 'relevant to me' and also one that understands the social issues girls today face at puberty."

The Creative Idea: Through research, Always learned that more than fifty percent of girls have a decline in confidence during puberty. This sparked what creatives call the "ah-ha moment," a nugget of research or a particular insight that becomes the key into connecting with the consumer. In this case, the point became to make Always a brand that empowers girls at a time when they are likely to be most vulnerable. Through creative brainstorming, one of the ideas that bubbled up was "like a girl" and all the ways that this term was used in a derogatory manner. The concept became how to turn that thinking on its head.

The Execution: The task was to change "like a girl" from an insult to inspiration. The creative execution first had to show the detrimental effects of using this term as a put-down, and then how Always could be a catalyst for changing that idea.

The video became the centerpiece for the campaign. Its purpose was twofold: 1) reposition the brand and 2) start a conversation, in particular via social media. As described above, the negative connotations are internalized by women, but through slight encouragement from the director perceptions can be changed—for them and for the viewer.

In addition to the video, the hashtag #LikeAGirl was introduced to spread the word via social media.

The Response: Globally, there were more than 85 million YouTube views of the film. According to Always, "Prior to watching the film, just 19% of 16–24s had a positive association toward 'like a girl.' After watching, however, 76% said they no longer saw the phrase negatively. Furthermore, two out of three men who watched it said they'd now think twice before using the 'like a girl' as an insult."[4]

4. *D&AD* (2016), Case Study: Always #LikeAGirl. Retrieved May 10, 2016 from http://www.dandad.org/en/case-study-always-likeagirl/.

Published reports claim that the campaign led to increased sales, but no exact figures are supplied, which makes me question the truth of that statement. However, P&G, Always' parent company, has had success with this strategy before, notably with Dove. Tying brands to social issues has become status quo, most particularly because millennials expect it.[5]

The following example is a bit more unusual because it is for a nonprofit cause rather than a brand. I include it here because the solution to the problem was not obvious and ultimately was quite ingenious.

The Brief: In 2013–2014, there were an estimated three thousand homeless people in Barcelona. The Arrels Foundation's goal is to reduce that number to zero. Homelessness is not a top-of-mind issue because there are no celebrities attached as with other social issues and because of the belief that it's the homeless person's fault that he or she is on the street. These people had become invisible.

Moreover, the point was not to get people to put money in the cup of a homeless person, but to get at the underlying problem. To make the invisible visible, the campaign had to introduce humanity into homelessness.

The Creative Idea: The goal was to come up with a social campaign that gives people something in return for their donation while integrating the street dwellers in the process and, ultimately, society. The team became inspired by the handwritten signs of the homeless. Handwriting is unique—as is each human being—and so the idea to

---

5. Mara Einstein, *Compassion, Inc.: How Corporate America Blurs the Line Between What We Buy, Who We Are, and Those We Help* (Berkeley: University of California Press, 2012).

create fonts based on individual writing became the basis for the campaign. How the fonts were developed, the individual stories of the writers, and how they are sold and used by different companies were the narratives that drew people into this issue. More important, the fonts are a product that is sold, raising money for the work of the foundation.

The Execution: Ten homeless men and women were selected for the campaign. Each had a different story to tell about how he or she ended up on the street, and these were turned into videos that were put on the project's dedicated website, HomelessFonts.org. The variety of experiences was used to convey the idea that living on the streets could happen to anyone, again working to humanize the homeless.

Typographers donated their time, and a font workshop was held to transform the writing into saleable fonts.

To perpetuate the campaign and provide maximum exposure, any time a company used a font from HomelessFonts.org it received a seal to put on the project. This gave the fonts more exposure while identifying the user as a socially conscious marketer.

The Response: HomelessFonts was launched in June 2014 with an initial five fonts. As more typographers came on board, that number has increased incrementally. According to the organization, "Within its first few months, HomelessFonts were purchased and downloaded by 307 organisations and individuals generating record proceeds and unprecedented empathy for the homeless people of Barcelona. Furthermore, the initiative attracted global media interest which, in turn, fuelled public support."[6]

6. D&AD (2016), Case Study: Homelessfonts. Retrieved May 10, 2016 from http://www.dandad.org/en/case-study-homelessfonts/

One final example is "Van Gogh's Bedroom," which not only provides the thought process from problem to execution, but also demonstrates the quantifiable success of the campaign and shows how old and new media can work synergistically:

The Brief: The Art Institute of Chicago owns the painting "Van Gogh's Bedroom." The museum wanted to create interest around a comprehensive exhibit of this work that would be displayed not as one but as all three versions of the work, the other two owned by institutions in Paris and Amsterdam. In addition to the paintings, the exhibit would include history about the works as well as a technological element. Importantly, it would only run for twelve weeks because the loaned paintings needed to be returned.

The Creative: Chicago ad agency Leo Burnett created a campaign that allowed people to experience Van Gogh's room. This included a room for rent as well as rooms created by local retailers. An important aspect of the creative was to produce a campaign that would generate a significant amount of earned media, an important element for a nonprofit that doesn't have a lot of money to spend on advertising.

The Execution: First, the agency placed posters in Chicago train stations advertising a room for rent. When people texted the number on the ad, they were engaged with Leo Burnett staffers responding as if they were Van Gogh, who texted back with information such as, "The apartment is not yet ready. Vacancies open 2/14. Text me back. We can talk existentialism and paint fumes." The room for rent—an almost exact replica of the Van Gogh paintings—was listed on Airbnb for $10 a night. This tactic was meant to create buzz, and it did. The room sold out in minutes, but also created 500 million media impressions, the equivalent of $6 million in media spending. Finally, a contest was held among local stores to create displays inspired by the Van Gogh paintings. Thirty stores participated, giving the museum additional visibility.

The Response: This campaign was so successful that the museum had its biggest opening weekend ever; daily attendance was 70 percent higher than projected, and the daily attendance for an exhibition was the highest in 15 years.[7]

Are there standard formats for print advertising?

For print ads, the traditional layout includes a large key visual, some text (called *copy*), a headline, and a picture of the product being sold, known as the hero shot. So, for example, an ad for Subaru will have a picture of the car prominently displayed in the ad, with a headline, some copy explaining the benefits of the car, and then a logo for the brand in the bottom-right corner. Alternatively, for a cosmetics company, the prominent visual will be a model or celebrity, there will be a tagline, and then the products will be pictured in the bottom right.

What about commercials?

Television commercials are produced as fifteen- or thirty-second spots. Within that short timeframe, advertisers attempt to tell a story about the product. There are a few different formats that they use to achieve this. Here are a few of the most popular.

Slice-of-life commercials show people in everyday situations where the product ends up being the hero of the story. This is also known as problem/solution advertising—you have

7. Jessica Wohl (April 7, 2016), "Want to Rent Van Gogh's 'Bedroom'?" *Advertising Age*. Retrieved May 10, 2016 from http://adage.com/article/creativity/art-instti/303425/.

a problem and voila! Our product will make it go away. Older examples here are McDonald's "You deserve a break today" or the Life cereal commercials that proclaimed, "Give it to Mikey. He hates everything," but then it turns out he likes Life cereal. Problem: Too busy to make dinner. Solution: Take the family to McDonald's. Problem: Your kids won't eat breakfast. Solution: Bring home Life cereal. Today, as in the past, these ads are particularly popular with laundry detergent advertisers or other household cleaners. The P&G "Moms" campaign is slice-of-life advertising.

Lifestyle ads present the user more than the product. These ads convey the idea that if your life is like this, then our product is for you. MasterCard's "priceless" campaign is a good example of this. In this case, it makes perfect sense to show what the product can do for you rather than the product itself. Apple has also used this format successfully. After all, the company doesn't spend time in commercials explaining the benefits of its technology.

A final example here is the Volkswagen "Darth Vader" ad from the 2014 Super Bowl. In this commercial, a young boy of five or six is dressed up as Darth Vader. He roams an obviously upscale home—there are large washers and dryers and an oversized kitchen, and mom is able to stay at home and make lunch for him. Throughout the house, he dramatically points his arms at objects in an attempt to make them do his bidding, but to no avail. Finally, dad pulls into the driveway and enters the house. The kid runs out to the car and points his arms toward the vehicle. As if by magic, the car's ignition is started, much to Darth Vader's surprise. The shot then switches to the kitchen, where we see dad in the kitchen with the key fob starting the car. This ad works on a number of different levels. First, it conveys the lifestyle of the prospective consumer. Second, it demonstrates that this is a family car without outright saying so. Finally, the commercial suggests that the car has new technological features (automatic ignition), again without screaming this in the consumer's face.

Presenter ads use a person to present the product to you. This is often a celebrity (Ellen DeGeneres for CoverGirl or Jennifer Aniston for Smart Water), or it could be a corporate executive like Frank Perdue. The presenter can also be a character, such as Flo for Progressive Insurance or Isaiah Mustafa for Old Spice in the "The Man Your Man Could Smell Like" ads.

Testimonials use satisfied customers to explain what they like about a product. In television, this type of advertising has fallen out of favor because no one believes that the endorser isn't being paid. Online, however, endorsers (also called *influencers*) are widely used because they perpetuate sharing through social media.

Demonstration ads present how a product is used while communicating its unique benefits. The best example of this would be the old Timex ads that claimed the watch "takes a licking but keeps on ticking." Today, as noted earlier, Microsoft demonstrates the advantages of its Surface Pro computer by showing artists using the pen to write on the tablet and claiming, "I couldn't do that with Apple." Demonstration ads are less common today because consumers tend to be more cynical of advertising than in the early days of television.

How is creative execution changing because of digital marketing?

Digital has turned the process on its head. Marketers create ads in a few days or a few hours, not a few months. They revise their ads instantaneously based on data they have about what prospective consumers click on. In the past, marketers would test their concepts with focus groups in several markets around the country. Today much of that work is done online. On Pinterest, for example, a marketer might put up an ad with two different pictures, track which one gets more clicks, and then promote the more popular execution through social media. This process replaces the focus group and it exists in a real-world setting. Because of this, some marketers do 20 percent of their work up front while 80 percent happens through revising and testing online.

Marketers also feel compelled to produce content constantly. Running just one well-thought-out ad doesn't work in the online environment; quantity is key. Part of this need to constantly put out content relates to the needs of search engine optimization (SEO), which means having an advertiser's content appear organically at the top of the Google search. An important way to do that is to consistently churn out content. Constant content also helps to increase consumer engagement, which is important for developing good customer relationships.

But how to produce all this advertising? It can't all be done by an agency or the client, so a number of different types of outside firms have proliferated. Content marketing firms like Newscred, Contently, or Scripted maintain stables of thousands of freelance writers, producers, designers, videographers, and photographers. Marketers can hire these firms to produce video and written content. In addition to content companies, other firms assist with one or more aspects of the workflow process, distributing content to the appropriate outlets and/or analyzing consumer engagement. Big names here include HubSpot, Percolate, Sharethrough, and Marketo.

With the need for constant content, art department bullpens are fast becoming glorified newsrooms. Overseeing the process is an editor or content marketer, who replaces the role of the creative director. The editor oversees strategy, writing, and consistency of message. Designers and contributors replace art directors and copywriters. In addition, there are two new roles: the SEO/paid specialist and the community manager. The first are media managers inasmuch as they oversee paid content (i.e., advertising) and they use this in conjunction with organic content to achieve SEO. Community managers represent the face of the brand; they learn who engages with the brand, they interact with community members, and they push content through social channels.

What other new strategies have gained popularity because of digital?

Lifestyle branding, experiential marketing, and influencer marketing have changed how campaigns are executed.

What is lifestyle branding and how does that affect execution?

Consumer brands from Always to Target to Coca-Cola need to articulate how they fit into their audience's lifestyle. Always is not about puberty, but empowerment. Target is not a store, but a destination for food and fashion. Coca-Cola is not merely a fizzy drink, but a stimulator of happiness in whatever setting it is added to.

Lifestyle branding takes branding one step further. In addition to the logo, tagline, and story, the brand gets more fully fleshed out through narratives and experiential marketing to allow consumers to see how products connect with their life and their values. This tactic has taken off because traditional cultural institutions no longer hold sway the way they used to. Instead of being defined by our jobs, our families, or our faith, now we can come to be defined by Starbucks, Apple, and REI. These products help consumers to communicate their values. Laurence Vincent of strategic branding company Siegel + Gale noted: "We use brands to validate our lives. A lot of our consumption activities are becoming more sacred because we attach meaning to them."[8] This is why TOMS Shoes, the company that gives away a pair of shoes for every pair bought, has remained popular for the last decade. Buying these shoes allows millennials to tap into their sense of philanthropy. Other socially conscious brands include Warby Parker and Seventh Generation, and some people would include Whole Foods

8. Christine Birkner (February 28, 2011), "Lifestyle Brands Make It Personal," *American Marketing Association.* Retrieved July 20, 2015 from https://lifestylebrandsblog.files.wordpress.com/2012/04/marketing-news_lifestyle-brands1.pdf.

on this list. Companies whose products or businesses don't innately communicate social good embed it into the product through their marketing efforts. That's what we have seen with Dove and Always connecting their brands to empowerment. Other examples of lifestyle brands include REI, Harley Davidson, Apple, Under Armour, and Ralph Lauren.

Lifestyle branding moves beyond the product and its advertising into experiences. In part, this can be attributed to the growing understanding that happiness comes from experiences, not things. The more a company can connect its product to a happy experience, the more connected the consumer will be to the brand. Moreover, within digital media, marketers connect with consumers on a one-to-one basis, making branding more personal.

What is experiential marketing?

Marketing campaigns—particularly those targeting younger audiences—increasingly have a real-world interactive element attached. Consumers don't just want to know what a brand stands for; they want to fully engage with it. This can occur in a number of ways. Mastercard, for example, markets its product as being a purveyor of priceless experiences. This began with an advertising campaign in the late 1990s. The copy would read: "Two tickets: $28. Two hot dogs, two popcorn, two sodas: $18. One autographed baseball: $45. Real conversation with 11-year-old son: priceless. There are some things money can't buy. For everything else, there's Mastercard." Today, the priceless events are sponsored live events, and a few card users even get access to musical stars like Justin Timberlake and Gwen Stefani. Thus, the narrative is not about the interest rate on the card or that you might get cash back, but about all the adventures you can have (without mentioning that you are putting it on credit or how you will pay for these expensive ventures at the end of the month— that's just not the point).

Budweiser's #upforwhatever is another good example here. Millennials who submitted an audition tape and promoted the brand via social media could be selected for the experience of a lifetime. Those lucky few who were picked were whisked away to an undisclosed location for a weekend of three-day partying with celebrities, fun, and beer.[9] It is no longer enough to see people drinking in a bar; one has to experience the ultimate party.

Millennials are not the only target for these campaigns. Marketing to teens today is more about experiences than about product attributes. Sour Patch Kids was a brand that was seeing steady growth but was still relatively small in terms of market share within the soft-and-chewy candy category. The company needed to do something out of the ordinary to make an impact in the market.

Mondelez International, the candy's parent company, took a three-pronged approach: increase its social media presence, produce relevant and ongoing video content, and enter into the music business. The brand created its marketing around the concept of "fame": uniqueness, connection to famous people, and having a distinct online presence. Online, this meant launching a Snapchat account and having Logan Paul, a social media celebrity, create content for it with the product's mascot. In addition, the brand sponsored Nickelodeon's 2015 Teen Choice Awards, during which the company had a parallel social media presence and, separately, created a custom emoji board made up of sour and sweet "Kidmojis." Beyond social media, the company created video content in conjunction with four time periods of importance to teens: Valentine's Day, prom, summer, and Halloween. The company created

9. Jeff Fromm (October 7, 2014), "The Secret to Bud Light's Millennial Marketing Success," *Forbes*. Retrieved March 11, 2015 from http://www.forbes.com/sites/jefffromm/2014/10/07/the-secret-to-bud-lights-millennial-marketing-success. Doritos had a similar event where they drove millennials to Las Vegas for a spur-of-the-moment weekend.

a contest on Snapchat for Valentine's Day wherein the winner's love story was turned into an animated film that was distributed on Instagram. The company also produced scripted content for YouTube using teen celebrities from that site as the leading actors. Finally, the company inserted itself into the music industry by creating houses in three musically influenced cities—Brooklyn, Austin, and Los Angeles—where rising music artists could stay while on the road. The houses were designed as high-end and included a recording studio and camera crews—as well as visible Sour Patch branding. The artists would then post a tweet to their fans about their experiences, which provided marketing for both them and the candy.

Between 2010 and 2015, the brand doubled its market share and more than doubled retail sales (from $120 million to $248 million). In 2014 to 2015, when this marketing effort was in full effect, sales rose by almost $30 million. As a follow-up and to keep the momentum going, Sour Patch Kids ran a casting call in Los Angeles to find people for a web-based reality series based on high school proms.[10]

An increasingly common form of experiential marketing is retail outlets devoted to a single brand. There's the ubiquitous Apple Store and now an increasing number of competitive Microsoft stores, the M&Ms store and the Hershey's store, as well as numerous pop-up stores promoting products from Asics athletic wear to the breakfast treat Pop-Tarts. In an interesting twist, Samsung opened an "unstore" in a trendy section of New York City. The 40,000-square-foot space is a high-tech showplace for Samsung Galaxy phones and virtual reality headsets. What you cannot do at the Samsung store is buy anything. This is experiential marketing taken to the nth degree. These concept stores *are* the advertising. Customers can test the products, ask questions, and gain a better understanding of the brand all without feeling like they are being pushed into a purchase.

10. Zach Brooke (April 2016), "15 Flavors of Fame," *Marketing News*, pp. 12–13.

The number of companies using this concept is expanding quickly. Target has an Internet of Things store under its regular store in San Francisco. Tory Burch opened a store for her sports line that features yoga classes and interactive displays for games and shopping. And even Amazon—yes, the online retailer—has used pop-up stores and is looking at permanent brick-and-mortar locations.[11]

What do you mean by influencers?

Marketers want to connect to people with a large following on social media. People like Lady Gaga, for sure, but also Instagram and YouTube celebrities. If these people endorse an ad to their fans, it creates visibility for the brand without being an outright sell. Sometimes these influencers are paid and sometimes they are not; it is often hard to tell the difference.

Is creating controversy a good creative strategy?

It can be, particularly if the company is prepared for the response.

Honey Maid graham crackers have been around for almost one hundred years. In 2013, the company determined that it needed to reposition the brand from being an old-fashioned household staple to a modern snack appropriate for today's families. The company hit on the concept of "wholesome" and tied that to the product and to families. In the ad, they show the crackers being eaten as part of S'mores or as Teddy Graham bite-sized crackers straight out of the box. The hook to modernize the product was the diverse and multiethnic range of families presented. We see a single dad with his son, a mixed-race couple with their three children, a military family, a heavily

11. Adrianne Pasquarelli (April 05, 2016), "Welcome to the 'Unstore' of the Future: Retailers Go Experiential," *Advertising Age*. Retrieved May 13, 2016 from http://adage.com/article/cmo-strategy/unstore-future/303342/.

tattooed dad playing drums while the mom and child dance around the living room, and a gay couple with their baby. Over these heartwarming scenes of hugs and happiness is a voiceover saying, "No matter how things change, what makes us wholesome never will. Honey Maid. Everyday wholesome snacks for every wholesome family. This is wholesome."

The company knew that featuring these families would cause a controversy, and it did. The company was boycotted and called sinful by right-wing conservative groups. But Honey Maid was ready with what some have called the most brilliant response ad ever. It was not really an ad, but an online video that responded to the vitriol spewed in relationship to the on-air commercial. The company asked two artists to print out all of the negative tweets and posts and roll them up. Stacking them up next to one another, they created the word "Love" in script on the floor of a loft. Surrounding the negative posts were the positive messages that had been received—ten times more than the hate. In a touching visual, the video shows hate being transformed into love.[12] The video was so moving that it was shared 270,000 times and had 3.5 million views in just four days, with only $6,000 in paid media.

What is the most important thing an ad has to do?

Get your attention. If the advertiser can't get you to watch the ad to begin with, it doesn't matter what it says.

I've heard that using animals and babies is the best way to get attention. Is that still true?

Yes, using animals and babies still works. For the latter category, E*trade effectively used a talking baby for years. In another popular commercial, babies appear to breakdance

---

12. Honey Maid: "Love," *YouTube*. April 3, 2014. https://www.youtube.com/watch?v=cBC-pRFt9OM.

on roller skates for Evian, suggesting that drinking more of this beverage brings out the youthfulness in everyone. As for animals, Budweiser regularly uses its Clydesdales and added more furry friends to the lineup to evoke compassion from viewers—especially female viewers—during the 2015 Super Bowl with its "Lost Dog" commercial. In the spot, an adorable white pup gets mistakenly locked into a truck that drives him off the ranch and away from the Clydesdales (and his very handsome owner). The commercial shows the puppy jumping out of the truck, trekking across muddy fields, and finally encountering a wolf a short distance from his home. As ominous music plays, we hear the horses banging to get out of their stalls. The horses protect the puppy from the wolf and the puppy is brought home and given a bath by his owner. It is almost impossible to watch this ad without crying.

Another immensely popular ad from 2015 was a spot for Android called "Friends Furever." This commercial shows a number of different mismatched pairs of animals—a dog and a dolphin, a monkey and a horse, an elephant and a sheep. As the animals romp and play, we hear a song called "Robin Hood and Little John," which is from Disney's animated movie *Robin Hood*. The video ends with "Be together. Not the same." Ads like these are becoming more popular because they evoke emotions that drive viewers to share the advertising.

Does sex sell?

No. Sex will get your attention, but it does not provide a unique selling proposition.

5

ADVERTISING AND SOCIETY

What is the leading criticism against advertising?

Too much advertising tops most critics' lists. Advertising is
everywhere. Commercials interrupt television programming.
Circulars weigh down our Sunday newspaper (if you still read
one). Banner ads gunk up the online environment while pre-
roll ads keep you waiting for YouTube videos. Ads pollute our
physical environment, from highway road signs to the overwhelming lights of Times Square to logos pressed into the sand
of beaches. There is barely a bathroom, a classroom, a mall, or
an airport that is a haven from commercial messages.

Other criticisms are that ads contain too much sex, perpetuate negative racial and gender stereotypes, and include
some people (white upscale folks or people that sort of look
like them) and exclude others (notably the poor, the old, and
minorities). There are too many ads for high-calorie foods
and sugary soft drinks, and too many of those target kids.
Ads promote materialism and suggest that a high-spending,
product-filled lifestyle is the ultimate life achievement, instead
of saving the planet or helping one's fellow man. I could go
on and on. Bottom line is that advertising contributes to how
we see the world, and marketing has edged into almost every
facet of our lives. If you don't believe this, know that the idea
of an engagement ring was created by the diamond industry,

and McDonald's is the main purveyor of food education in the country. Even so, these messages do not have to define us, especially as we become more aware of how to engage with advertising on our own terms.

How does advertising impact television programming?

Primetime television is "a world overwhelmingly populated by able-bodied, single, heterosexual, white, male adults under forty"[1] while the idealized image of women on television is white, underweight, and under 30, with plenty of disposable income. There is one very good reason why this latter group dominates the screen: they represent the sweet spot of advertisers' target audience. The dominant representation of women is right in the middle of the "female aged 18 to 49" demographic; it is exactly the women advertisers want to see, and more importantly sell to.

Do we really see thousands of ads every day?

I began this book by saying that we see three thousand, or maybe even five thousand, ads per day. That number has been bandied about by marketers and academics for decades. It has been used so often that it is accepted as common sense. But is it true? Researchers are beginning to think maybe not.

Those thousands-per-day figures have been attributed to Yankelovich Partners, a highly respected research firm, although no one has been able to find the source of the statistic. It seems the CEO of Yankelovich gave a speech to the Association of National Advertisers in 2004 outlining people's attitudes toward advertising. The findings showed that negative feelings about advertising had gotten considerably worse

---

1. K. Heintz-Knowles, J. Henderson, C. Glaubke, P. Miller, M. A. Parker, and E. Espejo, *Fair Play? Violence, Gender and Race in Video Games* (Oakland, CA: Children Now, 2001).

since the American Association of Advertising Agencies had asked the same questions in 1964. Sixty-one percent of respondents felt that "marketers and advertisers don't treat customers with respect; 59 percent feel that most marketing and advertising has little relevance to them; and 65 percent think that there should be more limits and regulations on marketing and advertising."[2] There were many other gloomy numbers for advertisers, but nothing about the number of ads we see. Yet this study became the source for "three thousand ads a day." The information has been quoted in publications from the *New York Times* to *USA Today* to Inc.com.[3]

So how much advertising do we see?

Research from Media Dynamics, Inc. (MDI), a media and advertising research firm, suggests that our advertising exposure is considerably less. While media consumption has almost doubled since 1945 (5.2 hours versus 9.8 hours today), advertising exposure has not increased commensurately. MDI attributes this to the many options available for avoiding ads. Rather than five thousand ads, we are exposed to 360 ads per day across TV, radio, the Internet, newspapers, and magazines, and of those, only 150 to 155 are ones we actually notice.[4] These numbers, though, do not include advertising exposures such as packaging we see in stores or the many ads that appear

2. "Consumer Resistance to Marketing Reaches All-Time High, Marketing Productivity Plummets, According to Yankelovich Study." Press Release. *BusinessWire*. Retrieved May 27, 2016 from http://www.businesswire.com/news/home/20040415005038/en/Consumer-Resistance-Marketing-Reaches-All-Time-High-Marketing.
3. Choice Behavior Insights (n.d.) "The Myth of 5,000 Ads." Retrieved May 23, 2016 from http://cbi.hhcc.com/writing/the-myth-of-5000-ads/.
4. Sheree Johnson (September 29, 2014), "New Research Sheds Light on Daily Ad Exposures," *SJ Insights*. Retrieved May 23, 2016 from https://sjinsights.net/2014/09/29/new-research-sheds-light-on-daily-ad-exposures/.

outside of our homes, such as in subway turnstiles or bus stops or even the flight attendant announcing that the airline will be serving Starbucks coffee. While I am willing to admit that "thousands of ads" appears to be too high, a few hundred is probably too low.

The issue, however, isn't the exact number of ads that we see but the fact that we are seemingly overwhelmed by corporately biased content. We obviously don't like it or we wouldn't be working so hard to avoid it. And as bad as it is for adults, it is worse for children. Kids from 2 to 11 years of age see more than 25,000 commercials per year, and half of that advertising is for fast food, candy, and cereal.[5] If you don't think there is a correlation between that and the childhood obesity epidemic, think again.

Can companies lie in advertising?

It is illegal for companies to lie to consumers. An advertiser who makes a claim of fact in an ad must back it up with research. This does not mean that the marketer might not fudge the truth. In a famous example, RJ Reynolds made the claim for Camel cigarettes that "More doctors smoke Camel than any other cigarette." This was in 1946, when cigarette smoking was widely acceptable, although health concerns were starting to be raised that would obviously have a negative effect on sales. To combat that, Camel used doctors—or rather men dressed as doctors—and put them in advertisements that included copy touting these trumped-up assertions. The company hyped that the information was supported by independent research surveys based on responses from thousands of doctors. Not so: the survey was conducted by the company's ad agency and the doctors were questioned in their offices and at medical

---

5. Federal Trade Commission Bureau of Economics Staff Report (June 1, 2007), "Children's Exposure to TV Advertising in 1977 and 2004," D.J. Holt, P.M. Ippolito, D.M. Desrochers, and C.R. Kelley, p. 9.

conventions, right after they had been handed a complimentary carton of Camels.[6]

What if an advertiser gets caught in a lie?

When advertising is outright spurious, the U.S. Federal Trade Commission (FTC) may be asked to look into the situation. This is true for many of the misleading weight loss products that show unrealistic results. However, it is not usually the advertising itself that leads people to complain to the FTC; rather, it is specious charges on their credit card brought about because of an automatic payment plan. Alternatively, consumers can bring class-action suits, which if proven can lead to multimillion-dollar settlements. In one example, Airborne—an herbal supplement created by a schoolteacher to keep away bacteria and germs—claimed it helped prevent colds and the flu. Well, not really: there was no research or any evidence of the product's efficacy. The Center for Science in the Public Interest sued, and while the company did not admit to wrongdoing, it did provide refunds to people who had purchased the product, which cost the company $23.3 million.[7]

The government and the courts are not the only recourse. Consumers can call marketers to task, and social media have facilitated that. Two examples come to mind. Coca-Cola, a major culprit in America's childhood obesity problem, tried to claim that its products were part of a healthy lifestyle. Consumers quickly responded—one even hijacked the video and replaced the voiceover with more truthful copy—and the

6. M.N. Gardner and A.M. Brandt (2006), " 'The Doctors' Choice Is America's Choice': The Physician in US Cigarette Advertisements, 1930–1953," *American Journal of Public Health*, 96(2): 222–232. Retrieved May 27, 2016 from http://doi.org/10.2105/AJPH.2005.066654.
7. Karlee Weinmann and Kim Bhasin (September 16, 2011), "14 False Advertising Scandals That Cost Brands Millions," *Business Insider*. Retrieved May 26, 2016 from http://www.businessinsider.com/false-advertising-scandals-2011-9?op=1.

campaign was summarily pulled.[8] Or, you may remember when Starbucks tried to enter the discussion of race relations by asking baristas to write "Race Together" on cups of coffee and to talk with customers about race relations. The angry tweets and social posts shut the campaign down in days.

What if the ad isn't lying, but it's not really honest either?

This is called *puffery*, and it is completely legal. Puffery is subjective ("We have the best coffee in Seattle") rather than objective ("Our coffee is 50 percent caffeine").

Advertisers are like magicians; they show you a beautiful, shiny object so you won't look at the man behind the curtain. That's what puffery and branding do; they make the product seem better than it is. We look at athletes and the swoosh but don't see the child labor that went in to making the Nike sneaker. We smile about a Happy Meal but don't think about the abysmal nutrition and the plastic toy that will end up in a landfill. We use Airbnb and never think about the hotel workers who are losing their jobs because Hyatt and Hilton have to live up to regulatory standards that individual homeowners do not.

Let's look a little closer at Airbnb and see how puffery plays out. A New York campaign for the company consisted of commercials and subway posters. One of the commercials, for example, showed an African American woman (to be read as low income) happily renting out a room in her home. Subway posters were divided in half; on the left side was a picture of a "typical New Yorker" and on the right side was the following headline: "New Yorkers agree: Airbnb is great for New York City." The body copy read: "Airbnb provides supplemental income for tens of thousands of New Yorkers. It also helps the local businesses in our neighborhoods and strengthens our communities. Airbnb is great for NYC." That last line is

8. The Coca-Cola ad can be viewed at http://www.youtube.com/watch?v=6r_9HPzMZTU, and "Honest Coca-Cola Ad" can be viewed at http://www.youtube.com/watch?v=bHhCP5ad-zM.

puffery because it is also not really true—but it is still legal for Airbnb to say it.

What is interesting to note about this campaign is that it wasn't targeting consumers. It didn't say "rent a room from Airbnb" nor did it say "here is how you can sign up to rent out a space in your home"—and, seriously, real estate is so expensive in New York you'd be hard pressed to find someone with an extra room to rent anyway! This advertising was a PR campaign to fight back again the state's attorney general, who found that 72 percent of the rentals were illegal and the vast majority of rentals were not in poor neighborhoods where the service might help supplement incomes (as suggested in the advertising) but in gentrified neighborhoods where people who owned multiple apartments were further lining their pockets. As the report noted, "Ninety-four percent of Airbnb hosts offered at most two unique units during the Review Period. But the remaining six percent of hosts dominated the platform during that period, offering up to hundreds of unique units, accepting 36 percent of private short-term bookings, and receiving $168 million, 37 percent of all host revenue."[9] These ads appeared in 2014, but the fight continues today. In late 2015, Airbnb purged a thousand "potentially illegal" listings from its New York offerings before the release of the data to the public. The concern on the part of the city and the state is that large numbers of apartments are being used for short-term rentals rather than permanent residents—something that affects local housing costs and reduces the tax base.[10]

9. Kevin Montgomery (October 16, 2014), "Attorney General: 72 Percent of Airbnb Rentals in NYC Are Illegal," *ValleyWag*. Retrieved May 24, 2016 from http://valleywag.gawker.com/ attorney-general-72-percent-of-airbnb-rentals-in-nyc-a-1647224530.
10. Noah Kulwin (February 10, 2016), "Did Airbnb Purge Potentially Illegal NYC Listings Ahead of Its Own Data Dump?" *Recode*. Retrieved May 24, 2016 from http://www.recode.net/2016/2/10/ 11587752/did-airbnb-purge-potentially-illegal-nyc-listings-ahead-of-its-own. For more on Airbnb, see also http://insideairbnb.com/.

Why do you need to know this? Because while puffery is legal, it may not be honest.

What are some of the underlying assumptions of advertising and what are its consequences?

Advertising, and more broadly consumerism, is built on the ideology that more is better, growth is good, and the "good life" means having ever more consumer goods. We can see why this is so. For more than a century, we have been bombarded with the idea that the market can solve problems, from "ring around the collar" to what to have for dinner and even who will be our life mate. Other social institutions that might have had a say in defining the notion of the good life no longer have the influence they once did, nor do they have the megaphone that the marketplace does.

Tied to this is the belief that it is possible to have unending economic growth without consequences.[11] Every quarter, Wall Street looks to corporations to announce increased earnings—the higher the better. Even when companies proclaim significant growth, headlines proclaim that it isn't big enough. A *New York Times* headline read, "Google's Quarterly Revenue Rises, but Analysts Still Fret About Growth."[12] What that headline didn't say was that revenue rose 12 percent of $17.3 billion.

We can see the flaws in these assumptions. Environmentally, the planet cannot sustain the continual stripping of its resources to create new goods. Nor can we sustain the level of consumer waste our society generates. How many plastic toys end up in landfills? How many computers have been sent overseas to contaminate rivers and riverbeds and cause cancer in the children who pull electronics out of trash heaps to earn

11. Justin Lewis, *Beyond Consumer Capitalism: Media and the Limits to Imagination* (Cambridge, UK: Polity).
12. Conor Dougherty (April 24, 2015), "At $17.3 Billion, Google's Quarterly Revenue Rose 12 Percent," *New York Times*, page B7.

money? Never mind what plastic bags and bottles have done to our environment, or the fact that water (and possibly air)—what every human needs to live—may soon become a scarce resource. Environmental degradation is an externality—a cost incurred by business but not paid for—that can no longer be neglected. Just as tobacco companies ultimately had to pay for the externality of cancer, so too should companies pay for pillaging the earth.

Is there any way for companies to work outside of the quarterly reporting system?

A few companies have attempted to step out of the constraints of Wall Street to produce socially conscious products without being required to make shareholders' concerns their top priority. These are companies that practice social innovation and live by the triple bottom line of people, the planet, and profits. One way companies have been able to do this is by obtaining "B Corp" certification. In order to become certified, B corporations must meet a number of standards, including transparency in reporting their social and environmental performance as well as financial reporting. Once vetted, the company executives can make business decisions that are socially responsible but may not be the most profitable without fear of being sued by shareholders for not fulfilling their fiduciary responsibilities. If a B Corp is sold, these values are maintained because it must be transferred as a wholly owned subsidiary. This aspect of the program was key as a number of companies, such as Ben & Jerry's and Tom's of Maine, were bought up by larger multinationals who did not maintain their social missions.

Why should we be particularly concerned about the impact of advertising on children?

Unlike adults, children do not have the maturity or intellectual capacity to combat the advertising onslaught. Under the age of eight, they simply cannot differentiate between advertising and editorial content. Elmo or the golden arches for McDonald's, Word Girl or the red bullseye for Target: it's all the same to them. That marketers target children anyway is fairly reprehensible. While little is done to combat this in the United States, other countries have passed regulations against it. In Sweden, for example, television advertising cannot target kids under the age of twelve.[13]

Why has marketing to children proliferated?

From an economic perspective, kids' buying power has increased exponentially—in part because their parents and grandparents give them more money and in part because there are simply more of them. This combination led to the ever-increasing aggregate buying power of kids aged four to twelve, going from $4.2 billion in 1984 to $17.1 billion in 1994 to more than $40 billion in 2002.[14] More recently, ad agency Digitas pegged kids as a $1.2 trillion market, if you include not only what they buy but also the purchases they influence.[15] This is why companies spend $17 billion marketing to children. This number is stunning when we take into account that this increased from $100 million in 1983.[16]

Marketers talk about kids age six and up in terms of having "consumer autonomy," though it's hard to think of a

13. N.A. (May 29, 2001), "Sweden Pushes Its Ban on Children's Ads," *Wall Street Journal*. Retrieved May 24, 2016 from http://www.commondreams.org/headlines01/0529-05.htm.
14. Packaging Digest Staff (2013, October 16), "The Undeniable Influence of Kids," *Packaging Digest*. Retrieved May 27, 2016 from http://www.packagingdigest.com/packaging-design/undeniable-influence-kids.
15. Martha C. White (April 11, 2013), "American Families Increasingly Let Kids Make Buying Decisions," *Time*. Retrieved May 27, 2016 from http://business.time.com/2013/04/11/american-families-increasingly-let-kids-make-buying-decisions/.
16. Campaign for a Commercial Free Childhood. (n.d.). *Marketing to Children Overview*. Retrieved May 23, 2016 from http://www.commercialfreechildhood.org/resource/marketing-children-overview.

six-year-old as being autonomous about anything. Over the last decade the list of "autonomous products" has grown and continues to expand today. For example, when I was growing up, mom made dinner and you ate it. Mom also had the final say about the foods the household consumed. Today, kids influence 72 *percent* of the family's food and beverage purchases—a growing area of influence as more and more products are developed for this group. Kids have the most autonomy when it comes to buying toys, selecting entertainment like movies, and choosing their favorite fast-food establishment. While they have less autonomy in other areas, they may still influence numerous family purchases, including products like computers, cars, and vacations.

Part of kids' ability to readily influence purchases relates to sociological factors. Key among these are that both parents work in most families, there is an increase in parenting styles that engage children rather than tell them what to do, and parents who grew up as latchkey kids or children of divorce feel bound and determined that their children will not suffer the same childhood woes as they did. They want only the best and most luxurious for their offspring. Ralph Lauren for kids, Uggs, and Pottery Barn Kids are just some of the brands created to appeal to this market. The push for "more and better" is not limited to clothes and shoes; it also applies to more classes, more after-school lessons, more of the best of everything—especially if parents want their kids to go to the best colleges. Thus, both children and parents become immersed in a dance of consumerism focused on spending increasingly more money on products and services for kids, tweens, and teens.

How are children marketed to?

Television programming that blurs the line between where the program ends and the commercial starts has come back into vogue. In the 1980s, regulations were in place that forbade the production of long-form commercials like *Strawberry Shortcake* or *Teenage Mutant Ninja Turtles*. Today, the rules no longer exist. And it's not just television: movies targeted to children have exploded in the last decade. Marvel films, Disney movies, DC Comics, Pixar, *Harry Potter*, and so on have all taken off because of the changing economics of the industry. Adults may go see a movie once, but if a child likes a movie, the DVD or download is sure to follow, as are the backpack, lunch box, books, toys, and other ancillary products. And as if these weren't bad enough, now there's *The Lego Movie, Transformers*, and dozens of Barbie movies that go direct to video.

Content is not the only tool: advertisers also use online gaming environments, called *advergaming*, to engage youngsters with their products. Products from Happy Meals to Lucky Charms to Coca-Cola create online worlds where kids spend untold amounts of time, with little awareness that it is an advertiser who has crafted the message. Note that all of these are food products, which are of particular interest to marketers because food is something kids both buy with their own money and influence others to pay for. By 2006, food marketing to children had gotten so out of hand, and the obesity issue had become such a major concern, that the industry began regulating itself—only because companies knew the government would be more restrictive. In 2013, researchers found that the fast-food companies did not follow the self-regulating guidelines, noting that they focused on the toys and movies being promoted rather than the food, which is misleading.[17] On the media side, the Disney Channel said it would no longer accept junk-food advertising as of 2015. Nickelodeon did not take the same steps

17. Maureen Morrison (August 28, 2013), "Study Slams Industry Self-Regulation and Kids' Marketing," *Advertising Age*. Retrieved May 26, 2016 from http://adage.com/article/news/study-slams-industry-regulation-kids-marketing/243888/.

to help kids.[18] In another example of gaming for marketing purposes, the National Football League was promoting
fantasy football games to kids aged six to twelve. The "NFL
Rush Fantasy" offered weekly prizes for the highest scores.
Although parental consent was required, kids could easily
bypass it. Even worse, the NFL created a school curriculum
to entice kids to play fantasy football. While the league has
not stopped promoting this very adult activity to kids, it has
eliminated the curricular materials.

What I have covered here merely skims the surface of the
issue. The Campaign for a Commercial Free Childhood (http://
www.commercialfreechildhood.org/) is an excellent resource,
and there are more included in this volume's appendix. One
last thing to note here, however, is the ability of advertising to
influence gender identities and to present overly sexualized
stereotypes. Girls in particular are encouraged to project a certain image and achieve a prescribed body type. Disney prin-
cesses and Barbie dolls come to mind here. The next question
addresses the consequences of this.

What is the interconnection among women, body image, and advertising?

In the United States, there is a national obsession with weight
and body image that has been steadily growing for five
decades. Watch any television talk show or read any woman's
magazine, particularly in January when resolutions are made
or in April leading into "swimsuit season," and you will see
endless diet and exercise programs. These products are so
popular (and profitable) because women (and increasingly
men) have been obsessing about weight since Twiggy hit the

---

18. Hollie McKay (July 1, 2013), "Disney Dumping Junk Food Ads, But
    Nickelodeon Still Says No," *FoxNews.com*. Retrieved May 26, 2016
    from http://www.foxnews.com/entertainment/2013/07/01/disney-
    dumping-junk-food-ads-but-nickelodeon-still-says-no.html.

fashion scene in the 1960s. Fifty years later, the U.S. diet and exercise industry rakes in $60 billion a year.

The weight loss and fitness industry has employed a variety of strategies to promote the use of its products and services: getting one's figure back after having children, implementing scientific-sounding terminology like "cellulite" (a term coined by *Vogue* to sell magazines), or focusing on health and wellness in response to the "obesity epidemic." One new strategy is to use advertising messages with thinly veiled communications of faith. For example, when Jennifer Hudson was the spokesperson for Weight Watchers, she told viewers "I believe . . . I was strong before, but I'm stronger with Weight Watchers." For an African American community steeped in faith, one could easily substitute "Jesus" for "Weight Watchers." Not surprisingly, when her contract was over, she was replaced by Oprah Winfrey, who embodies a similar spiritual frame.

Driving the need for all this dieting are the images of overly thin models and actresses in magazines, on TV, in movies, and in advertising, which all work in conjunction with one another to prod us to achieve a size that has no basis in reality. On average, U.S. models stand 5-foot-11 and weigh 117 pounds, which means that the majority of fashion models are thinner than *98 percent* of U.S. women.[19] And that's the *average*-size model! When was the last time you stood next to a woman who was 5-foot-11, never mind one who was 117 pounds? The answer is probably never. That's because the average U.S. woman is 5-foot-4 and 140 pounds.

Two things happen when we see these funhouse pictures over and over again. First, because actresses and models are on television or in a magazine, we confer on them a higher status.

19. R.D. Gina Jarman Hill (2009), "Media Images: Do They Influence College Students' Body Image?" *Journal of Family and Consumer Sciences* 101(2): 28; L. Smolak, "Body image," in J. Worell and C. D. Goodheart (eds.), *Handbook of Girls' and Women's Psychological Health: Gender and Well-being across the Lifespan*. Oxford Series in Clinical Psychology (pp. 69–76) (New York: Oxford University Press, 2006).

We believe they must be more important, more virtuous, or somehow fundamentally better than we are or they wouldn't be on the screen or the page to begin with. We imbue those in the media with an aura of "specialness" that we want to have. The ridiculousness of this is brought home by reality shows like *The Bachelor*. Would you subject yourself to the humiliation of not being selected by a guy (and usually not a very nice one at that) in front of millions of people? Maybe you wouldn't, but millions of people would—just for the chance to be on television.

The other thing that happens is that we come to see media images as not only the feminine ideal, but also the female norm. It's hard to remind ourselves that most women don't really look like Gisele Bündchen or Jennifer Lawrence or any of the women from *Game of Thrones* when that's what the media present day after day. These images and ideas skew our view of reality. And that's the point: for the vast majority of women and girls the issue isn't how much we weigh, it's our *perception* of how much we weigh. There's nothing wrong with our bodies; it's our *body image* that's out of whack.

Some statistics tell the story. Nine- to eleven-year-old girls are more likely to say they are unhappy about the way they look than six- to eight-year-old girls (78 percent versus 68 percent). This is not just an age phenomenon: while how much girls dislike their looks increased by ten points, for boys that number was up by only three points. And girls are more likely than boys to see themselves as overweight even though boys are the more overweight sex. According to a national survey of high school students, 29 percent of boys and 22 percent of girls were overweight or obese, but only 23.3 percent of boys considered themselves to be overweight or obese while *34.9 percent of girls considered themselves to be overweight or obese*. At the same time, 28.8 percent of boys and *62.3 percent* of girls said they were trying to lose weight.[20]

20. CDC. 2002. YRBSS, 2001, Table 34. *MMWR: CDC Surveillance Summaries* 49 (No.SS-5):1–94. Retrieved November 21, 2016 from http://www.cdc.gov/mmwr/preview/mmwrhtml/ss4905a1.htm.

While we wish it were not so, girls *are* more invested in their looks than boys. They are more likely to care about their weight and to care about what others think about them. They are also more likely to do something about it, either through dieting or plastic surgery, which are products and services that advertisers are happy to sell them.

Attitudes about weight and dieting begin at increasingly young ages. Girls as young as six and seven are concerned about becoming fat and by age ten 81 percent are afraid of being fat. [21] Fifty-one percent of nine- and ten-year-old girls feel better about themselves if they are on a diet. [22] And 46 percent of nine- to eleven-year-olds are "sometimes" or "very often" on diets, while 82 percent of their families are "sometimes" or "very often" on diets. [23] By the time girls get to college, dieting has become a way of life; 91 percent of women recently surveyed on a college campus had attempted to control their weight through dieting. [24] All this is evidence to support that we learn very young to dislike the bodies we are in and we continue to do so throughout our lives: 80 percent of American women are dissatisfied with their appearance. [25]

The way in which women are portrayed in advertising and media affects how girls see themselves physically. In a recent

21. L. Mellin, S. McNutt, Y. Hu, G.B. Schreiber, P. Crawford, and E. Obarzanek (1991), "A Longitudinal Study of the Dietary Practices of Black and White Girls 9 and 10 Years Old At Enrollment: The NHLBI Growth and Health Study," *Journal of Adolescent Health* 20(1): 27–37.
22. Ibid.
23. A.M. Gustafson-Larson and R.D. Terry (1992), "Weight-Related Behaviors and Concerns of Fourth-Grade Children," *Journal of the American Dietetic Association* 92(7): 818–822.
24. Kurth et al. (1995) quoted in "Perfect Illusions: Eating Disorders and the Family," *PBS*. Retrieved May 27, 2016 from http://www.pbs.org/perfectillusions/eatingdisorders/preventing_facts.html.
25. L. Smolak (1996), *National Eating Disorders Association/Next Door Neighbors Puppet Guide Book*. Retrieved May 20, 2016 from https://www.ndsu.edu/fileadmin/counseling/Eating_Disorder_Statistics.pdf.

study,[26] girls were shown pictures of a spectrum of athletic women—sexualized athletes, performance-focused athletes, sexualized non-athletes, and non-sexualized non-athletes— and asked to complete a survey. Researchers found that seeing performance-based women created less body shame in girls than the more sexualized female depictions. Thus, seeing women doing something makes girls feel better about themselves. Another important finding of this research was that heavy readers of magazines showed more shame and concern about their bodies. This supports earlier research that discovered that 70 percent of the college women felt worse about their body after reading a magazine.[27] Now we understand why: the vast majority of photographs in these magazines show girls as sexual objects rather than actors in their own lives. The same negative feelings are now being seen after people spend time on Facebook, only now women are competing not against some unattainable, unknowable model but with their friends and family members.

In sum, as represented by the media, girls and women look virtually the same, they like to shop, and they are interested in having lots of sex. What we don't see are powerful women of different sizes, with varying interests, who are successful in multiple areas of their life.

Does marketing affect social institutions in addition to individuals?

Yes. The consumer mindset has become so pervasive that it has seeped into areas where it never previously existed, and few

26. Elizabeth A. Daniels (2006) "Media Representations of Active Women: What Are Girls Seeing and Does It Affect Their Self-Concept?" Unpublished PhD diss., University of California, Santa Cruz.
27. Stanford University News Service (March 1, 1993), "College Women Love, Hate Their Women's Mags." Press release. Retrieved May 27, 2016 from http://news.stanford.edu/pr/93/930301Arc3380.html.

if any major institutions have not been affected by it. Here we will look at the impact on higher education and religion.

How does marketing change the way we think about universities and what is the impact on higher education?

It's no secret that college has become the Holy Grail for an increasing number of Americans. While in 2000 there were 15.3 million college students, by 2012 the number was 21.6 million—more than ever before. We've all heard the familiar reasons why: expanded college capacity starting in the 1960s that never contracted, the "dumbing down" of high school and the younger grades, and the large number of people between the ages of eighteen and twenty-four (the millennials). But an important and less examined reason for the rapid rise in college enrollment is the increased use of marketing in the field of higher education.

Just as there is little difference between Crest and Colgate, Fructis and Finesse, except for the marketing, now the same holds true for colleges and universities. *US News & World Report*'s ranking of colleges has driven the milquetoasting of higher education. Once happy to create different curricula based on faculty expertise and student interest, now universities are forced to develop their course offerings to answer to the guidelines of the annual rankings. If not, they risk falling into obscurity. (Note: The crème-de-la-crème schools are partially exempt from this because of their brand status. However, even they answer to market pressures, though less so than the less vaunted institutions that cater to millions of students.)

In response, universities must create ways for their institution to stand out from all the rest. Part of that has to do with changing the product. For some, it means bigger buildings and better science labs. For others, it's opulent sporting arenas or amenities that rival a Canyon Ranch spa. One thing you won't see them promoting is their teaching. That's because undergraduate academics—the thing you are supposedly buying—is an area few colleges care much about, though that appears to be changing, as I discovered on recent trips to universities while "shopping" for my daughter.

It is impossible to know exactly how much money is spent on marketing higher education, but we know that administrative costs are increasing far more than the cost of faculty, and much of that is allocated to marketing and development. There are conferences dedicated to marketing higher education, including one sponsored by the American Marketing Association, and marketing consultants for colleges are on the rise. Nothing is more telling about the importance of marketing, though, than the creation of the higher education chief marketing officer (CMO), a title that has begun to flourish only in the last ten years.

Why the need for this top-level sales executive when the colleges can practically sell themselves? Marketers exist to improve sagging reputations in light of the high cost of education and all the bad publicity around increasing debt levels—something we can thank Ronald Reagan for, because he reframed education as an individual good rather than a social one. Government support was therefore changed from grants (which don't have to be repaid) to loans (which do). Selling the idea of marketing within a university is not an easy balance. Educators don't want to think of students as "customers," so branding is euphemistically called "identity." No matter what you call it, however, the reality is that from direct marketing materials to tweets to alumni emails, marketers are managing the message to solidify the equivalent of a corporate identity.

Branding the university is important to influence three constituencies. First, the colleges need to attract the best and brightest students. Second, branding helps to attract alumni money. Colleges invest heavily in consumer relationship marketing (CRM) to reach prospective students, but they also use this to create and maintain loyalty to the institution over a lifetime, the same as any consumer product. Finally, college branding is used to attract funding. Corporations work with universities to create named professorships (the Walmart chair of marketing) and provide funding for research.

Consumer companies also want access to colleges because they are target-rich environments for new consumers. Students are an extremely important target for marketers, who clamor to attract the attention of this very distracted cohort. From technology to cellphone plans to credit cards, marketers want to establish a foothold with this age group so that when they have graduated and are paying the bills, they will stick with the brands they are used to. One of the reasons why students have such easy access to credit cards on college campuses is because the credit-card companies gave kickbacks to the universities, which so desperately needed the funding that was no longer coming from the government.

The workings of the university have begun to mimic those of business and consumer culture, the so-called corporatization of the university. We see this in how the colleges and students interact with one another. During the first few weeks of the semester, students "shop" for classes. Students sign up for many more classes than they could ever take and then drop the ones that have the hardest syllabus or seem less interesting in person than they did in the course description. Students think of themselves as consumers of education, and who can blame them? They approach college like every other investment. This is fully brought home when they review professors like they would a restaurant. Every college has its internal rating system that other students use to shop for a class in subsequent semesters. These ratings are also used in tenure and promotion decisions, so professors who are up for tenure tend to be easier on students in an attempt to improve their ratings. Then there is the very public Rate My Professor, a website owned by one of the best marketers of all, MTV.

The problem is that education isn't designed to give consumers what they want; it is meant to get young people to think and reevaluate their belief systems. This is a process that is bound to make them uncomfortable and thus is one that doesn't fit well within the consumer model.

What is the impact of marketing on religion?

Religion in the United States is different from in other countries. The First Amendment to the U.S. Constitution prohibits the establishment of a national religion. In so doing, the country was set up to have a vigorous marketplace for the practice of spirituality because different religious practices would have to compete to attract believers. This was unlike most European or Latin American countries, where a majority of the population participated in the state-mandated faith, such as the Church of England in Britain or Roman Catholicism in Brazil. This market competition also helps explain why religion is still widely practiced in the United States, while it is not in many other industrialized nations.[28]

Marketing religion is not new.[29] From Jehovah's Witnesses going door to door to ads in Sunday newspapers, religion has long been promoted. What is new is a confluence of events starting in the 1960s that has moved religion from being a marketed service to being a commodity product that can be readily bought and sold. First, there is no longer a social stigma attached to not attending religious services. In the past, churches were the hub of community life, providing social connection and news of local goings-on. If one did not show up on Sunday morning, it would be noticed. But as we moved from an agrarian society to a metropolitan one, people were more likely to establish community affiliations through their work life as that consumed more of their time and energy. Second, religion has become something that is attained rather

28. Mara Einstein, *Brands of Faith: Marketing Religion in a Commercial Age* (London: Routledge, 2008).
29. R. Laurence Moore, *Selling God: American Religion in the Marketplace of Culture* (New York: Oxford University Press, 1994).

than ascribed—that is, people choose their faith rather than it being determined for them. Traditionally, if your mother was a Baptist, for instance, then you would be a Baptist too. No longer: after the civil disruption of the 1960s, baby boomers sought to break with the older generation, and a key means of doing that was to decide on their own religious beliefs. Not only did boomers choose their own faith, they began combining faiths ("JuBus"—for Jewish Buddhists, for example). This has been given the derogatory name "cafeteria religion."

Finally, it was not enough to know that one could choose a faith; people also had to know what alternatives were available to them. By the 1980s, and even more so in the 1990s and 2000s, the widespread availability of cable television and its televangelists and then the Internet with a wealth of religious options—from the Vatican to the Church of the Blind Chihuahua—allowed spiritual "seekers" to test out different belief systems without having to make the very public commitment of walking through the doors of a local church.

Thus, the elimination of social stigma, the ability to choose one's faith, and readily available alternatives led to the phenomenon of shopping for religion, which turns religion into a product like others we have discussed. And with this commodification of religion comes marketing, and increasingly branding, of religions themselves. For example, the Church of Latter Day Saints (the Mormons) has been running a campaign called "I'm a Mormon" for a number of years. The campaign includes television commercials and outdoor billboards with the express purpose of driving people to the church's website. There, visitors can "meet a Mormon" and then interact with the person through social media—a form of digital evangelism. The key message of this campaign is that Mormons are "just like us."

The Mormons are not alone. Campaigns exist for the Methodist Church ("10,000 doors"), Scientology ("Know Yourself. Know Life"), and the Episcopal Church ("Transforming Churches"), among others. Even ISIS, though it is an ideology rather than a religion, has taken some of the best tools for marketing faith and used them to attract new recruits.

Some of the best marketers are televangelists—preachers who promote the faith via television. The most popular by far is Joel Osteen, pastor of the Lakewood Church— the country's largest megachurch,[30] with close to 50,000 weekly congregants—and the author of a number of bestselling books, including *Your Best Life Now*. In addition to his many books, he has a weekly television show that reaches more than seven million viewers through a combination of cable and broadcast TV outlets. His website (joelosteen.com) provides live streaming of weekly services and has archives of previous ones. In addition, Joel—and part of his branding is that he is known as Joel, as opposed to Pastor Osteen, so as to appear approachable and friendly—regularly goes on tour to promote the faith, and, well, his books, TV show, online service, and even the live church service (which is held in a former basketball stadium that holds more than 16,000 people). All of these strategies work synergistically with one another to sell the brand that is Joel Osteen.

While not a televangelist, another important pastor in the megachurch category is Rick Warren, the leader of the Saddleback Church in California and the author of *The Purpose-Driven Life*—the highest-selling nonfiction book after the Bible. Warren has famously promoted how he brought traditional consumer marketing tools to the practice of faith. Specifically, he went door to door to ask people if they went to church, and if they did not he asked why. He learned that people wanted shorter services and messages that meant sense for their life. He also introduced psychographics—understanding people through values and lifestyles rather than demographic statistics—into the marketing strategy, deciding to target

---

30. Megachurches are defined as having two thousand or more regular congregants. More than 50 percent of regular church attendees go to a megachurch.

"unchurched Harry," an upscale male who is unlikely to attend church because he doesn't want to be hit up for money or be asked to serve on another committee. Thus churches began to look like shopping malls and community centers, often including basketball courts, networking classes, and a Krispy Kreme. Others took note of Warren's success and tried to replicate it in their local congregations, some going so far as to enlist the aid of Disney consultants to create the best environment to attract religious shoppers.

Through all of this, religion has become a product—a commodity—that can be bought and sold in ways that are no different from selling cornflakes or an iPod. In fact, most religions have attempted to create a brand for themselves. Many see the branding of religion to be increasingly important in order for religious institutions to remain part of the cultural conversation. And the reality is that if institutions don't market themselves, the market will find ways to take advantage of religious and spiritual forms and beliefs. There is still hesitation, however, on the part of traditional institutions, who view marketing as suspect and unnatural. However, others have determined that marketing religion is similar if not identical to evangelizing. And given that marketing in the online space is so inexpensive relative to traditional media, more institutions are accepting marketing as "part of doing business."

Why do marketers use philanthropy to get us to buy?

In an earlier chapter, we talked about the head sell and the heart sell. Today, marketers talk about a spiritual sell. Called Marketing 3.0 by marketing professor Philip Kotler and his colleagues, this new thinking derives from marketers' realization that consumers are driven by values: "Instead of treating people simply as consumers, marketers approach them as whole human beings with minds, hearts, and spirits. Increasingly, consumers are looking for solutions to their anxieties about making the globalized world a better place. In a world full of confusion, they search for companies that address their deepest needs for social, economic, and environmental justice in their mission, vision, and values.... Marketing 3.0 complements emotional marketing with human spirit marketing."[31] This suggests that the market has filled the void left by people's move away from institutionalized religion. They have turned to the market to help them express their value system.

How does promoted philanthropy play out in the marketplace?

Pink. Lots and lots of pink. Read any woman's magazine or watch a television show during the month of October and you can't help but be overwhelmed by a propensity of pink—ads for pink puffer jackets, pink bracelets, I've even seen pink drill bits. Saks Fifth Avenue offers a "Key to the Cure" t-shirt, Ford Motor Company promotes "Warriors in Pink" gear from print ads to product placement, all while promising "100% of the net proceeds from each sale supports one of four breast cancer charities." No less than the NFL wraps itself in pink, with players wearing pink armbands and pink sneakers, and the ubiquitous pink ribbon even adorns major league football fields.

Why have so many companies attached themselves to the breast cancer charity bandwagon? Because it's simple (for many companies it means simply putting a pink ribbon on a package); it demonstrates the company's philanthropic side (which we know is important to millennials and, in the case of the NFL, distracts people from thinking about domestic violence problems within the league); and these promotions target women (the purchasers of 80 percent of consumer goods).

31. Philip Kotler, Hermawan Kartajaya, and Iwan Setiawan. *Marketing 3.0: From Products to Customers to the Human Spirit* (Hoboken, NJ: Wiley, 2010.).

Is this cause-related marketing?

Yes, and breast cancer is just the tip of the iceberg. Over the last decade female-friendly charities that connect philanthropy to product purchases have proliferated, particularly those related to health, childhood education, or the environment. This is known as *cause-related marketing*, and while it used to be a goodwill tool used by PR departments (P&G has had a longstanding relationship with the Special Olympics, for example), now it is a sales mechanism implemented by marketers (buy this candy bar and 5 cents will go to charity). Estimates are that in 2010 cause marketing was used by 75 percent of brands, and 97 percent of "marketing executives believe it is a valid business strategy."[32] Cause-related marketing is so widespread because associating products with charities sells more products. Period. According to the *Cone 2010 Cause Evolution Study*, "85% of consumers have a more positive image of a product or company when it supports a cause they care about" and "forty-one percent of Americans say they have bought a product because it was associated with a cause or issue in the last year." For consumers there are a number of advantages: the charity helps justify paying for high-end products; socially conscious brands have become tools in identity creation, so buying one of these products tells the world you are a caring person (think Livestrong bracelets); and buying a product attached to a cause allows consumers to cross charity off their to-do list.[33] Improved sales are not the only benefit to companies. Most campaigns have a social media element that enables the company to capture consumer data, and since these

32. "New Study Reveals: Men Really Do Have a Heart," *Barkley*. Press release. Retrieved May 14, 2011, http://www.prnewswire.com/news-releases/new-study-reveals-men-really-do-have-a-heart-106647888.html.
33. Mara Einstein, *Compassion, Inc.: How Corporate America Blurs the Line between What We Buy, Who We Are, and Those We Help* (Berkeley: University of California Press, 2012).

campaigns are now advertising and thus a deductible business expense, they help to reduce the company's tax burden. A corporate win-win-win.

For charities, however, all is not so well. Many have questioned how much money is actually going to the charities. Ambiguous language, such as "net proceeds," doesn't tell consumers anything about how much of their hard-earned cash is actually going to help with research or to aid the less fortunate. More pointedly, while raising money and raising awareness are good, they do not lead to any substantial social change that might help with the underlying issue. The homeless commercial in the previous chapter, for example, attempted to do both.

To put this into perspective, let's look at the history of this technique. The first cause-marketing campaign was implemented in 1983 by American Express to raise money to restore the Statue of Liberty. Donations were based on how much money people spent on their Amex cards during the fourth quarter of that year as well as for new cards issued. The campaign received positive media coverage and raised $1.7 million. However, let me draw your attention to the timing of this event. Throughout the 1980s, the Reagan administration systematically cut corporate taxes. With smaller government and less revenue, the social safety net was effectively gutted. Since the federal government no longer supported many charitable organizations, they turned to corporations in an attempt to fill the void. While corporations did increase their philanthropic giving, these funds could not make up for the monies the government no longer supplied.[34]

Two shifts occurred that changed how cause marketing was executed. First, in the 1990s, companies were looking to increase efficiencies and improve profits. In line with this, cause campaigns had to be aligned with strategic marketing objectives, such as increasing sales, opening markets, or creating partnerships with nonprofits. This meant that campaigns

34. Sophia A. Muirhead, *Corporate Contributions: The View from 50 Years* (New York: The Conference Board, 1999).

moved out of PR groups and into marketing departments. The second major shift occurred with the proliferation of social media. These platforms enabled companies to use word of mouth to spread their messages, because while people might not share a straight sales message, they would share information connected to a charity. We share information related to causes we care about, first because it is easy—spawning the word "slacktivism"[35]—and second because it conveys to the world that we are good people. The marketer gets positive endorsements while gaining information about consumers.[36]

Shopping, however, will never be about making the world a better place. You may feel better about buying high-priced items, and an important charity may get some needed exposure and a few dollars. However, if we scratch the surface of many causes we will find larger social issues. Lack of food is about lack of jobs to pay for it. Joblessness is increasing due to technologies that are replacing human workers, many of whom cannot be retrained to participate in the new economy. These problems take political action, not a trip to your local store.

How is advertising used in politics?

Advertising and politics is an area of study unto itself and can cover anything from electoral politics to issues-based campaigns like those related to the food industry or abortion to the marketing of violence and the promotion of fear as a political issue (think President Donald J. Trump). Two of the main

35. Kirk Kristofferson, Katherine White, and John Peloza (2014), "The Nature of Slacktivism: How the Social Observability of an Initial Act of Token Support Affects Subsequent Prosocial Action," *Journal of Consumer Research* 40(6): 1149–1166.
36. Mark Andrejevic, *ISpy: Surveillance and Power in the Interactive Era* (Lawrence: University Press of Kansas, 2007); "Service and Social Media: You're Not Social (Enough)," *DestinationCRM.com*. Retrieved April 2, 2011 from http://www.destinationcrm.com/Articles/ Editorial/Magazine-Features/Service-and-Social-Media-Youre-Not-Social-(Enough)-54785.aspx.

criticisms against the marriage of advertising with politics are 1) the use of negative advertising, like the famous Willie Horton ad during the Dukakis/Bush campaign, the Swift Boat ad attacking John Kerry's military service, or, frankly, most ads during the Clinton/Trump matchup, and the consequences this has on current and future political discourse, and 2) the cost of advertising, which is what has driven the need to raise so much money in U.S. politics. Eliminate the need to pay for advertising and you eliminate (or at least minimize) the ability of wealthy people to influence the outcome. Interestingly, researchers and a limited number of pundits acknowledge that political advertising—like most advertising—is ephemeral at best.[37] Ads presented months in advance of an election likely do little. Rather, it is ads immediately before the election and, more important, the ground game of talking with people one on one (the equivalent of word-of-mouth marketing) that ultimately make the difference.[38] In light of the recent U.S. presidential election, individually targeted social media ads directed at undecided voters in the last few days are certain to be an area of intense study, in terms of both their effect as word-of-mouth marketing and their ability to quash voter turnout. It is impossible to cover the full implications of advertising in politics within in this space.[39]

37. John Wihbey and Denise-Marie Ordway (February 6, 2016), "Negative Political Ads and Voter Effects: Research Roundup." Retrieved August 17, 2016 from http://journalistsresource.org/studies/politics/ads-public-opinion/negative-political-ads-effects-voters-research-roundup.
38. Andrew Cockburn (April 2016), "Down the Tube: Television, Turnout, and the Election-Industrial Complex," *Harper's*. Retrieved August 17, 2016 from http://harpers.org/archive/2016/04/down-the-tube/. See also WNYC, On the Media (April 12, 2016), *Magic 8 Ball* (radio show). Retrieved August 17, 2016 from http://www.wnyc.org/story/on-the-media-2016-08-12/.
39. For more information on political advertising see: Erika Franklin Fowler, Michael M. Franz, *Political Advertising in the United States* (Boulder, CO: Westview, 2016); Shanto Iyengar, *Media*

Can emotions, specifically happiness, be marketed?

In the case of happiness, yes. Marketing happiness has grown exponentially, leading to what William Davies has called "The Happiness Industry."[40] Davies suggests that this is not new, but the latest forms have become pervasive. Gretchen Rubin's book *The Happiness Project* found a massive audience and led to a monthly column in a popular women's magazine. The success of Oprah was built on how women would be happier either through makeovers or books or free cars. And one of the most popular courses at Harvard is on positive psychology, known as the Happiness Course. But marketing happiness is more about putting us in the mood to buy than in making us feel good about ourselves. Remember, advertising is about attaching emotions to products and services—the happier we are in relationship to a product, the more likely we are to buy. Really smart, right?

What is particularly pernicious about this is that the pursuit of happiness has become a way for marketers to co-opt and commoditize yet one more area of our lives. We have long known that it is not objects that make us happy but rather experiences.[41] Experiences like watching a sunset or talking with a loved one are what make us happy, and they are free.

Why do we have a fascination with hoarders?

In the first chapter, I mentioned reality shows about hoarders. This genre has proliferated to include shows like *Hoarders,*

Politics: A Citizen's Guide (New York: W.W. Norton, 2016); Alexa Robertson, *Media and Politics in a Globalizing World* (Malden, MA: Polity, 2015); The Annenberg Public Policy Center (https://www.annenbergpublicpolicycenter.org/political-communication/); Wesleyan Media Project (http://mediaproject.wesleyan.edu/).

40. William Davies, *The Happiness Industry: How the Government and Big Business Sold Us Well-Being* (New York: Verso, 2015).

41. Jesse Singal (August 12, 2014), "How to Buy Happiness," *New York Magazine*. Retrieved May 27, 2016 from http://nymag.com/scienceofus/2014/08/how-to-buy-happiness.html.

Hoarders: Family Secrets, and *Hoarding: Buried Alive.* We get the same feeling watching these shows as we do watching the *Biggest Loser,* but instead of "I would never let myself get that fat" the internal dialogue is "I would never buy that much stuff." Hoarders became a salve for justifying our own purchases. And while it is true that your house will never be filled to the rafters with garbage, you very well might go to The Container Store and buy big plastic containers to hold a bunch of stuff that you stick in your closet or your basement or at a storage facility and never look at again. The real question, the final question to ask about advertising and society is this: *Why did you really buy that (fill in the blank) and what could you have done instead?* It will save you money and space and very likely the planet.

6

MEDIA

ADVERTISING'S EVERYWHERE

How do marketers decide where to advertise?

Media selection is about taking the right message produced by the creatives and putting it in the *right place at the right time in front of the right people.* The "right place" is any medium from television to radio to magazines to the Internet where the target audience—the "right people"—spend their time. The "right time" entails understanding when the consumer or prospect is going to be most receptive to the advertiser's message. So for example, if P&G is selling Pampers, the company is looking to put its message in front of mothers, who are primarily in their late twenties or early thirties. Primetime programming, such as *Grey's Anatomy*, is a good choice, as is *A Baby Story*, a reality series about having a newborn. *Parenting* magazine and mommy blogs also fit this target audience. On the other hand, MTV attracts many women within that age range, but putting a quiet, cuddly commercial about babies next to *Catfish*, a show about dating scams, is not appropriate. In another example, if a marketer is looking to target young men, late-night TV, sports programs, and *Maxim* are sure to be part of the media plan.

What is media planning?

Media planning is the creation of a detailed blueprint outlining the timing of media (by year, week, and day), what media will be used, and how much media will be employed.

Before this can be done, a number of issues and questions need to be addressed. First, is this a product that is sold throughout the year? Most products have some seasonality and therefore will need to be advertised more heavily at different times during the year. Let's use the example of engagement rings. Key times when people get engaged are during the end-of-year holidays, Valentine's Day, and in the spring when love is in the air. But marketers shouldn't advertise on Valentine's Day—that would be too late. They need to advertise well before that time so the groom-to-be has the ring in hand. Therefore, Zales is likely to advertise from roughly October through the beginning of February and then again in April, May, and June. Advertising during certain times of the year and not others is known as *flighting*, and all advertisers use some form of this continuity strategy to maximize their budget and stretch the time over which consumers will see their message. Soda is another good example. Key sales periods include the Super Bowl, holidays like Memorial Day and Labor Day, summertime, and year-end holiday parties. Finally, if a company or category has promotional days or seasons, those also need advertising support. Beer and the Super Bowl or Bed Bath & Beyond and "off to college" promotions may come to mind.

There are additional time considerations to take into account: the time of day and day of the week. Dunkin' Donuts, for example, will advertise during morning news shows to remind people to pick up a "Cup A Joe" on the way into work. Boston Market will advertise during evening drive time on the radio to help mom decide what to serve for dinner. Movies are advertised on Thursday nights when people are beginning to map out their weekend plans. Beer and booze ads are shown during weekend sports programming.

In addition to timing, the planner needs to know if the product is sold throughout the country, and if the category or brand sells better in one area than another. After all, snow blowers will be sold in January in the Northeast due to seasonality, but they are never going to sell in desert states like Nevada. There may also be places where a product or brand is more popular than others. Companies determine this using a category development index (CDI) or a brand development index (BDI), which are simply percentages of category or brand sales over the size of a population in a given area. When I worked on Miller Beer, for example, we used to do a separate campaign in Texas in addition to the national campaign because such a large percentage of overall sales came out of that single state.

Next, media selection needs to be made based on the planner's best assessment of where to reach the target audience and whether or not that medium fits with the message being conveyed. Here, too, a number of factors are relevant. First, how much money does the client have to spend on the campaign? The size of the budget will affect everything from what types of media will be used to how many types will be employed. If the budget is large, television can be included. If the advertiser is working on a tight budget, digital media is likely to be the backbone of the plan. Ultimately, the target audience is the most important factor in determining where advertising will be placed. If the target audience is millennials, native ads on BuzzFeed and product placement in *Orange Is the New Black* might be on the plan; if the target is baby boomers, television will be the place to reach them. Finally, the planner must decide on the media mix—that is, the types of media used in the plan and how are they going to work in conjunction with one another to maximize message delivery. Television is great for reaching a large audience, but it can be expensive. Digital is inexpensive, but it takes a long time to reach a large group of people and sometimes it can be labor intensive. Magazines are good for beautiful visuals and engagement. Radio is great for reminders but has a lot of commercials, what advertisers call clutter. Deciding how to balance these issues is at the heart of the planner's work.

What is the difference between media planners and media buyers?

Media planners work with the account team and the creatives to determine the types of media that should be used for a particular advertising campaign and how much emphasis should be put on each media type. This is much of what was discussed in the previous question. Once the plan has been established, the media buyers negotiate with the sellers of media vehicles—individual television networks or magazines or radio stations—to get the best price for their clients.

What are the different types of media that advertisers use?

Media planning is nothing more than buying time and space. Time is bought on TV, radio, or online, and space is purchased in print publications such as newspapers and magazines as well as online as banner ads or splash pages. The chart below outlines the broad categories of media available.

Media Categories	
Broadcast	Television
	Radio
Print	Newspapers
	Magazines
	Out of Home
	Direct Mail
Nontraditional	Digital (online and mobile)
	Cinema
	Product Placement

While conceptually simple, media planning is not easy—far from it. Media planning has gotten significantly more complex over the last decade as audiences have become increasingly fragmented and new venues for advertising have appeared. In the 1960s, advertisers could put one commercial on a major network in primetime and reach 30 percent or more of the audience. Finding a large audience like that today is almost impossible. Viewers can timeshift—that is, record programs to watch on their own schedule. Instead of simply broadcast television, we have the option to watch network, syndication, or local television, plus network and local cable. We can also watch programming on demand, view it online or through apps, or choose alternative video outlets like YouTube. In addition to television, there are thousands of magazines reaching specialized audiences, and almost every day digital media have a new option to offer to advertisers, whether it's a new app or a new feature on existing apps like filters on Snapchat or live video on Facebook. Each new outlet means more fragmentation, more individualized viewing, and fewer ways for advertisers to reach a mass audience.

Because traditional media do not have the same efficacy that they used to, advertisers are putting more money into specialized communications that work in relationship to other media, including PR, sales promotion, and direct marketing, particularly via email.

Which medium is the most important for advertisers?

While we hear all about digital, television remains the most important medium. Even with the changes in viewing patterns, we spend equal amounts of time with television as we do with digital and more time with either of them than with other media. However, TV is the only medium to deliver a large audience, and it has the added benefit that most people (84 percent of Americans) watch television with a second screen.[1] Digital devices might be used to check Facebook or email, but they are also used to buy products: "Seventeen percent of consumers use secondary devices to purchase products

---

1. Greg Sterling (February 11, 2014), "Nielsen: More Time On Internet Through Smartphones Than PCs," *Marketing Land*. Retrieved February 3, 2015 from http://marketingland.com/nielsen-time-accessing-Internet-smartphones-pcs-73683.

featured on the programs they watch."[2] For the vast major of advertisers, commercials on television are the foundation of the media plan.

How do media planners know who watches a TV show?

Nielsen's TV ratings tell an advertiser who and how many people have watched a television show. Media planners are most interested in the age and gender of the viewers as well as their household income. This information is captured through People Meters. These meters look like a cable box and track viewing data in 25,000 homes across the United States, a group that is a representative sample of the U.S. population. Nielsen used to count only who was viewing a show at the time when it aired, but today, because of high DVR usage, they count C3: initial viewership plus anyone who watches a recorded program within three days. These rating numbers are important because the size of the audience affects how much the television network can charge for commercials.

People Meters track national ratings, though there are some local People Meters in larger markets. Incredibly, to track viewing in most local markets, Nielsen uses two million paper diaries.[3] These local ratings are assessed four times a year during sweeps—November, February, May, and July. You may be aware of these time periods inasmuch as the networks put all their best shows—cliffhangers, end-of-season weddings, results of *Dancing with the Stars*—on during these months in order to goose the ratings.

2. PR Newswire (May 28 2014), "2014 ARRIS Research Reveals Consumers Are Finding New Ways to Get Entertainment on Their Terms." Retrieved November 21, 2016 from http://www.prnewswire.com/news-releases/2014-arris-research-reveals-consumers-are-finding-new-ways-to-get-entertainment-on-their-terms-260870741.html.
3. Nielsen (n.d.) "TV Ratings." Retrieved May 16, 2016 from http://www.nielsen.com/us/en/solutions/measurement/television.html.

Media planners also rely on secondary data from Mediamark Research, Inc. (MRI). While Nielsen provides information about who is watching, MRI data provides demographic information on heavy and light users for a broad swath of products. This is important because the rule of thumb is that 20 percent of a product's users represent 80 percent of sales. Knowing who the heavy users are becomes the basis for defining your target audience. In addition to providing usage demographics, these reports include what TV shows and magazines these users watch and read. Based on this information, planners pick media vehicles that deliver their target audience.

How do media planners know who reads a particular magazine?

Magazines are assessed by the Alliance for Audited Media (AAM). This independent company verifies the number of subscribers plus how many people buy the publication on the newsstand—combined, this equals the circulation. Knowing newsstand sales is helpful to media planners because it allows them to get a sense of how healthy the publication is. If lots of people are buying a magazine from the newsstand, which is significantly more expensive than having a subscription, that's a good indication that the person is vested in the magazine and will spend more time reading it and perhaps engaging with the advertising. In addition to circulation, AAM estimates the readers per copy (RPC). While one person may have a subscription, multiple people are likely to read the publication. The number of people who read the magazine without buying it is known as the pass-along rate. For some publications, say *People* magazine, which is in most doctors' and dentists' offices, the pass-along rate can be considerable.

As mentioned, MRI data provides in-depth information about who reads magazines. Publications compile pertinent data and package it in a sales tool called a *media kit*, which includes the size of the audience, gender composition, composition by age groups (18–24, 18–49, etc.), median age, household

income, education level, employment—including whether
someone is in a professional or managerial position—and
whether there are children in the home. Examples can readily be found online. While television is used to reach a large
number of people, magazines are used to connect directly with
target audiences.

Are there other considerations beyond where to place the advertising?

Media planners need to balance reach, frequency, and continuity. Continuity has to do with staying in front of the consumer
as often as possible without overpromoting the product so
that people begin to tune it out. Frequency is the number of
times that someone sees a marketing message. It is believed
that someone needs to see a message three times in order to
grasp the communication. This is known as effective frequency. People don't need to see a *commercial* three times, but
they do need to see the *message*. Therefore, they could see a
commercial, an outdoor ad, and a pre-roll on YouTube, all with
the same communication. Reach is the percentage of the target audience that the advertiser wants to reach with its sales
message.

Media planners are also concerned about the efficiency of
a media vehicle. To determine efficiency, planners calculate
the cost per thousand (CPM). This is "the price for reaching
a thousand members of the target audience via the outlet."[4]
CPMs are used for all media and therefore can be used as a
comparative device for media selection. For example, if a television program reaches 10 million members of your target and
charges $200,000 for a 30-second commercial, then the CPM is
$20 per thousand. This makes television an efficient vehicle.

4. Joseph Turow, *The Daily You: How the New Advertising Industry
   Is Defining Your Identity and Your Worth* (New Haven, CT: Yale
   University Press, 2011).

On the other hand, magazines will have a higher CPM because they have a smaller audience. However, magazines may be less costly out of pocket.

What determines the cost of a TV ad?

An ad is priced based on the number of people seeing it (impressions) and who those people are. The bigger the audience, the higher the price. This is why Super Bowl commercials—a show with 100 million viewers or more—cost $3 million for a 30-second spot. But cost is not only about size. Advertisers want to reach certain groups of people (the target audience), some of whom are more valuable and expensive than others. Young men are especially hard to reach, so advertisers will pay much more to reach them than many female demographics.

Traditionally, ads on broadcast television were more expensive than cable television. It is easy to see why. Broadcasters had significantly larger audiences and so they could command high prices. Cable, on the other hand, had very small audiences. However, a number of cable networks were still able to extract high prices from advertisers because of the audience. Early on, MTV delivered a young audience that was hard to find elsewhere, and advertisers were willing to pay handsomely for that, though still not top dollar. More recently, while broadcast viewership has declined and original cable programming has improved, some cable shows have started to command similar prices. We saw this with *The Walking Dead*.

Surprisingly, the cost of broadcast advertising has not dropped even as ratings have fallen. *Seinfeld* consistently reached more than 30 million viewers, while *The Big Bang Theory* delivers half that audience. Even so, a 30-second commercial goes for nearly $350,000. Advertisers are willing to pay the higher cost for broadcast because it is still the only place to reach a significantly large audience that will see the advertising simultaneously. More recently, the networks have begun to reduce the number of commercials in their program to artificially decrease supply. This has fueled demand and kept prices up, as discussed earlier.

Cable networks are going to start to feel the pinch, too, as more Americans drop their cable subscriptions. Over the last fifteen years, cable homes have dropped from 70 percent to 54 percent of the United States.[5] "Cord cutters" and "cord nevers" are choosing to watch over-the-top (OTT) programming, like HBO Now and CBS All Access, as well as streaming outlets like Hulu, Amazon, and Netflix, which on its own accounts for twenty-eight hours per month of viewing per subscriber.[6] Forty percent of U.S. households have at least one video streaming service, according to Nielsen.[7] Fewer cable subscribers means fewer people watching the advertising, which means less money for the cable networks.

Is cost determined differently with other media?

No. Radio, magazines, and newspapers work under a similar model. The exception is digital, which will be discussed below.

Why is there a difference between broadcast and cable television advertising?

In the early days of television, broadcast TV was sent to your home via airwaves and captured by an antenna that sat on

5. Television Bureau of Advertising (2017). "National ADS, Wired-Cable & Broadcast Only Household Penetration Trends" Retrieved April 13, 2017 from https://www.tvb.org/Public/Research/CompetitiveMedia/CableADS/NationalADS,Wired-CableBroadcastOnlyHouseholdPenetrationTrends.aspx. The NCTA is the cable and telecommunications association used to present these facts. Of late, their website has become opaque and confusing, as if to obscure the industry's decline (see https://www.ncta.com/).
6. Jack Loechner (March 5, 2015), "Netflix To Grow Fourfold From 2010 to 2020," *Media Post*. Retrieved March 30, 2015 from http://www.mediapost.com/publications/article/244737/netflix-to-grow-fourfold-from-2010-to-2020.html.
7. Alexandra Sifferlin (March 11, 2015), "Americans Are Watching More Streaming Video and Less Live TV," *Time.com*. Retrieved March 30, 2015 from http://time.com/3740865/more-americans-streaming-television/.

the roof of your home, through which the signal was sent to your TV screen. At that time, each city (or "market" as Nielsen calls them because the area they track covers more than the city proper) would have only a handful of channels. These included the major broadcast networks—ABC, CBS, and NBC—and depending on the size of the market perhaps there would be two or three other local stations. In New York, the country's largest market, there was WNEW Channel 5 (which would later become a Fox affiliate), WOR Channel 9 (now MyNetwork), and WPIX Channel 11 (now The CW). In addition, there was the local PBS station beginning in the late 1960s, but this was noncommercial fare. Because of consolidation in the 1980s and 1990s and the creation of new networks like Fox and The CW, those independent channels have now become network affiliate stations. This underlying structure exists today but most people are unaware of it because they get their television signal via cable, satellite, or the Internet. It is important to understand this system, though, because it affects how advertising is purchased, and it is not the same for broadcast as it is for cable.

Major Broadcast Networks
ABC
CBS
NBC
Fox
The CW

Broadcasters produce programming at a central source (the network) and feed the signal to their affiliated stations in 200-plus markets around the country. These stations may or may not be owned by the network, and while the stations are incentivized to air all of the programming provided by the network, they are not required to do so. Additionally, the broadcast network does not provide programming for 24 hours per day, so the local station needs to fill those time slots with nonnetwork programming. Local news and sports or syndicated programming (reruns like *Seinfeld* or *The Good Wife* and first-run content like talk shows and judge shows) are used for this purpose. So, while ABC affiliates around the country will all be showing *Scandal* at 9 p.m. on Thursday, not every station will have the same show on at 4 p.m. Most of the commercials aired during network programming are national, with profits going to the network; local news, sports, and syndicated fare appear only in the local market, where profits go to the station.[8] This is why local news has expanded to so many more hours throughout the day.

Cable television is much less complex. Cable networks from MTV to CNN to Bravo send a signal up to a satellite. The local cable operator, such as Comcast or Time Warner, pulls that signal off the satellite and sends it through a cable to your home. People around the country will see the exact same programming throughout the day. The cable network inserts commercials into the programming and retains that revenue. Several minutes each hour are given over to the local affiliate, which in this case is Comcast or Time Warner, who can use that time to sell advertising to local companies.

How does the difference between broadcasting and cable affect how commercials are purchased?

Every May the broadcast networks trot out their stars and present the new lineup of shows to advertisers at what are known as the "upfronts." After the networks have wined and dined advertisers and wooed them with Kerry Washington or the cast of *The Voice*, the advertisers go back to their offices and begin to make bids on the show they want to advertise in. Buying time during the upfront market has a few advantages for advertisers. First, they can get what may turn out to be hit

---

8. Syndication is national. For more explanation, see http://www.museum.tv/eotv/syndication.htm.

programming for a steal. A 30-second spot on last year's mega-hit, *Empire*, sold for $139,200 as a midseason replacement during the upfront; a year later, a 30-second spot costs five times that amount. Second, during the upfront the advertiser gets a guarantee that the network will deliver the audience that it promised. So, if the advertiser is guaranteed 20 million women between 18 and 49 years of age, that is what the network must deliver. But what happens if the new *Empire* wannabe turns out to be a dud? The network then has to give the advertiser a "make-good"—that is, the network has to provide enough commercials (in different programming) to deliver the promised audience. If you have ever watched television and seen the same commercial over and over again during a short span of time, that is likely due to a make-good.

Seventy-five to 80 percent of the network inventory is sold during the upfront season. The remaining 20 to 25 percent is used for make-goods or is sold in the scatter market. Scatter market inventory is more expensive than upfront purchases and can be significantly more expensive if the market is tight, which happens during Olympic and presidential election years.

Cable networks also have upfront presentations and they sell, mostly, in a similar way. Broadcasters sell individual shows. Cable, too, sells advertising in individual programming, like *The Walking Dead* or *The O'Reilly Factor* or sports programming on TNT or ESPN. However, the remainder of the day on cable is sold as run of schedule (ROS). This relates to one of the other key differences between broadcasting and cable: broadcasters are trying to reach a large audience while cable networks are programmed to reach a specific demographic. When cable programming was widely introduced in the 1980s, it was envisioned as the magazine rack of television—one network for sports, one for news, one for kids, and so on. Because these networks couldn't depend on making money through large audiences like the broadcast networks, they had to do it by creating audiences that advertisers would highly value and therefore pay a premium price for. This explains the success of a network like MTV. MTV may not have a big audience by broadcast standards, but it attracts an important audience and one that is very hard to reach through traditional media. Therefore, advertisers will pay dearly to get their message in front of a teen/young-adult audience.

A major trend in advertising sales is platform selling. As discussed earlier, because of media consolidation, most media companies are made up of broadcast and cable networks in addition to other media properties. So NBCUniversal, which is owned by Comcast, has as its lineup NBC, Bravo, USA, Syfy, and E! among many others. Rather than selling these as separate entities, the company has begun to sell media plans that maximize delivery of a target audience across multiple outlets.[9]

What are dayparts?

Television and radio are broken down by daypart. You are likely aware of primetime, that daypart from 8 p.m. to 11 p.m., when television attracts the largest audiences. Other television dayparts include daytime, morning news, late night, and sports. Radio dayparts include morning drive, midday, and afternoon drive. As we can schedule programming based on our own preferences, these are becoming increasingly less relevant.

How has advertising changed with the introduction of digital technologies?

The most significant change with the movement to digital is the ability for marketers to track everything we do online. Every click, every search, every item dropped into an online shopping cart is followed by an advertiser or a marketing research

9. Jeanine Poggi (May 2, 2016), "Live from New York: One-Third Fewer Ads!" *Advertising Age* 87(9): 8.

company. Knowing exactly what you do online enables marketers to focus their pitch so that (in theory) you will only see ads for products and services you are interested in. A boon for the marketer is that digital advertising is much less expensive than advertising on traditional media, and digital is more specifically targeted so less money is wasted putting an ad in front of people who are unlikely to be interested in the product.

What is paid, owned, and earned media?

Advertising online is in one of three areas: paid, owned, or earned media.[10] Paid media is advertising. This could be a display ad, a banner ad, pre-roll on a website, or paid search. While in a traditional campaign this would have been the foundation of the plan, online it supports owned and earned media. Owned media includes any content "owned" by the marketer, which can include websites, blogs, mobile sites, and social media pages on Facebook, Instagram, YouTube, and so on. Paid media and owned media work to drive earned media, which is any form of "free advertising." Earned media can be anything from when we share content through social media to conventional PR techniques such as placing products on a blog or getting publicity on traditional media.

Understanding that the primary goal online is to generate social media buzz is fundamental to understanding the online environment.

What is big data?

Every time you click, type, or delete; every time you put a product in a shopping cart; how much time you spend on a

10. Sean Corcoran (December 16, 2009), "Defining Earned, Owned and Paid Media," *Forrester Research*. Retrieved March 10, 2015 from http://blogs.forrester.com/interactive_marketing/2009/12/defining-earned-owned-and-paid-media.html.

web page—this is all data that marketers use to gain information about you and how you shop. Marketers garner information from real-time listening and they analyze the pictures that are posted on social media to see what we are drinking with our Domino's pizza. With this data, marketers will send specially targeted ads to your tablet, cellphone, or computer. They may also use this information to improve their advertising by A/B testing—that is, testing one version of an ad against another to see which one gets more clicks.

Big data is simply an enormous set of information. Census data is a traditional example of big data. Through the digital realm, companies (and governments, as we know from Edward Snowden) amass huge stores of information based on the information we generate. Here are some stats: there are more than 1 trillion Google searches per year, and 1 billion users on YouTube (owned by Google) collectively upload three hundred hours of video per minute and have 4 billion views per day. Video usage is the same on Facebook, which means there are 8 billion video views per day on just two social sites! Facebook has 1.65 billion Facebook users, who "like" pages 4.5 billion times a day. Instagram and WhatsApp (both owned by Facebook) have 600 million and 1.2 billion monthly users respectively, Twitter has continues to hover around 300 million users, and Snapchat has 100 million active users. And these are just a few of the most popular social media sites: there's also LinkedIn, Google+, Pinterest, Tumblr, Foursquare, Vimeo, Flickr, SlideShare, StumbleUpon, and more added almost daily. But data is not only collected on social media; information is also snatched up when you shop on Amazon, listen to Spotify or Pandora, read *People* magazine, or visit websites from BuzzFeed to Salon to Refinery29, and so on and so on.

How does big data relate to ad sales?

Big data intersects with marketing in two key ways.

First, marketers can micro-target sales pitches based on where we are in the buying process, whether we are just starting to gather information or are putting the product into the cart, and they know where we are based on the data they have been collecting as we have moved around the Internet; this is our "click stream." As part of this individualized targeting, content is customized for the prospect. So if the customer is a college student, the ad she sees will include twenty-somethings and a storyline related to her lifestyle.

Second, marketers use our data to guess what products we will want. Every "like," retweet, post, and share signals to marketers who we are and what we intend to buy. Big data companies help marketers to collect, sort, and analyze this information in order to target the appropriate message to us. Even with all this information, however, they do not always get it right.

How do cookies work?

A cookie is code that is embedded on your computer. Data companies use this code to track you—or rather your computer—so that they can auction off your cookie to advertisers. This is done through ad exchanges (which function like the stock exchange). Say you go to Best Buy to check out the latest cellphone. While you are there, companies like Acxiom or BlueKai will embed a cookie on your computer. The ad exchange will auction off your cookie to advertisers looking to find people in the market for new cellphones. That might be Samsung or AT&T. The highest bidder gains access to display cellphone ads on your device as you travel around the Internet.

What is programmatic media buying?

Programmatic buying is purchasing advertising using computers. It works the same way that traders buy and sell stocks on Wall Street. It is widely used for online sales and has been slowly moving into other media.

How did the transition to programmatic occur?

As outlined thus far, media buying is a fairly straightforward process. Advertisers select media and negotiate for ads or commercials in individual media vehicles. After they run, they assess the ads' effectiveness based on Nielsen ratings or other research, and finally by evaluating sales figures. Based on all this, the plan will be adjusted accordingly. Within this framework, though, targeting is imprecise because Nielsen ratings are more of an educated guess than statistical fact. Also, a marketer who places an ad on primetime television to reach women 18 to 49 will also be reaching people who have no interest in that message.

Early on, web advertising followed a similar model. Banner ads were the first type of advertising created for the web. In the early days of the Internet, the websites themselves would produce static advertisements to appear on their site, much in the way a print ad would appear in a magazine. Banner ads were purchased the same way, too. The buying process stayed essentially unchanged even as newer formats appeared.

Google changed all that. Google was a forerunner in native advertising—ads that are indigenous to the platform in which they appear—before this even had a name. Believing that ads should be as useful as search results, the company produced its ads to look like the results of search queries: a small block of text with a link to the advertiser's landing page. These were much more successful than banner ads, which so few people looked at that the term "banner blindness" was coined. In addition to people looking at the ads, they clicked on them, enabling Google to track them. In the early 2000s, these were still being sold by sales reps using the traditional CPM model.

Ad sales began to change when Google introduced AdWords, which the company promoted by saying, "Have a credit card and 5 minutes? Get your ad on Google today."[11] Unlike television,

---

11. Scott Karp (May 27, 2008), "Google AdWords: A Brief History of Online Advertising Innovation," *Publishing 2.0*, Retrieved August 29, 2015 from http://publishing2.com/2008/05/27/google-adwords-a-brief-history-of-online-advertising-innovation/.

which needs big advertisers with big pockets, Google was going after smaller companies who might not be able to afford traditional advertising and needed to reach specialized audiences. Selling high-end musical instruments? Have first editions of Wonder Woman comics? AdWords allowed companies to reach highly targeted audiences interested in these products because the ads were sold based on a word search. Thousands of small businesses buying little bits of advertising—the "long tail" strategy made popular in the book of the same name—helped Google to create a sustainable revenue source. Note, though, that the CPM model was still being used.

The model took a fundamental shift in 2002 when Google introduced AdWords Select, a service that is based on a pay-per-click auction model. With this pay-per-click practice, advertisers pay only if a visitor clicks on the ad. If they do so, then the visitor is counted as part of the "click-through rate" (CTR), the percentage of people who go to the advertiser's landing page. Ad placement is done by auction. Advertisers bid against one another based on the price they are willing to pay. But price alone does not determine who wins the bid: the ad must be relevant to the search, and Google created mechanisms to make sure that would happen. According to Steven Levy in *In the Plex*: "There was one feature built in to try to ensure that the most useful ads would appear: advertisers couldn't pay their way to secure the best positions. Instead, the more successful ones—the ones that lured the most people to click on them and go to the advertiser's landing page— would get priority."[12] This ad quality formula is effective because, according to former vice president of global online sales Sheryl Sandberg, "it made the advertiser do the work to be relevant. You paid less if your ads were more relevant. So you had a reason to work on your keyword, your text, your

12. Steven Levy, *In the Plex: How Google Thinks, Works, and Shapes Our Lives* (New York: Simon & Schuster, 2011), pp. 85–86.

landing page, and generally improve your campaign."[13] And, finally, the auction is done by computer so that the assessment of relevance and bidding is performed and an ad is served in approximately 0.26 seconds.[14]

Selling via auction brought two important changes to media buying. When marketers buy search terms, they are paying for behavior (what we are searching for), not content (what we are watching or reading). Because of the ability to track us and collect data along the way, extracting media buying from the content in which it appears holds true throughout digital media. The biggest concern for advertisers online is to reach consumers as far down the sales funnel as possible. What that content is, then, is gratuitous. Let me be clear. We know that advertisers traditionally were looking for large audiences. They made educated guesses about who watched what TV programming and put their advertising dollars behind those TV shows. Today, companies place cookies on our computer, follow our IP address, and place an ad no matter where we are online. We could be watching National Geographic or cat videos; the content does not matter. If that is the case, there is little incentive to produce expensive or substantive programming or important news like investigative reporting.

There is another downside for us, the consumer. Think about it. Type "jeans," and The Gap or American Eagle appear, which is fine. But what happens when you type "depression"? More than likely, drug ads will populate your screen. This is not the same as seeing a pharmaceutical ad during a prime-time show when the advertiser thinks prospects are watching. The targeting is generic, not tied to an individual or an individual IP address. And while advertisers claim they only care about the behavior, not the individual, it is a bit disconcerting

13. Ibid., 92.
14. Christopher Ratcliff (October 30, 2014), "What is Google AdWords and How Does It Work?" *Econsultancy.com*. Retrieved August 18, 2015 from https://econsultancy.com/blog/65682-what-is-google-adwords-and-how-does-it-work#i.1iuztbw1504fas.

to think a company knows—or at least captures information about—a medical condition it attaches to you.

Second, auctioning space is used to buy any manner of advertising online. Auctioning space off automatically by computer is called *programmatic buying*. There are two types of programmatic buying, according to the Internet Advertising Bureau: direct and real-time bidding (RTB). Direct programmatic buying is like traditional ad buying in that the advertiser provides parameters based on cost and demographics and the space is guaranteed. The only difference is that a computer does the buying. RTB is the same as online auctions. In the same way that Google AdWords auctions opportunities to advertise, RTB is used across the web for display ads instead of search terms, and significant consumer data is involved.

What is the interrelationship among data brokers, ad exchanges, and programmatic buying?

Companies—so-called data brokers—collect, analyze, and package information about us and then sell it to advertisers. These companies used to be called direct mail houses and we called what they did database marketing. They sent you junk mail and catalogs. Today's digital version is called *customer relationship marketing*, and these companies gather information by following you around the Internet. With that information (some of which might be personally sensitive), they are able to feed you eerily specific advertising.

Amassing data—even large amounts of data—about consumers is not new. Magazine publishers and credit card companies have long collected information on their customers. Loyalty programs, like airline frequent flyer plans and store cards that you keep on your key ring, are all ways for companies to compile more specific information about what we buy, when we buy, and how often we travel.

Knowing that companies are collecting this kind of data may or may not bother you. Where people tend to get a bit antsy is when they think about companies poking into areas that are none of their business, such as the state of our health, how much money we make, and whom we are sleeping with. The problem is, we don't get to decide what does and does not get collected, packaged, and sold.

Marketers use consumer data to for inventory purposes and to target their promotions. In the first case, for example, Walmart tracked buying data to understand what people most need in the event of a storm. Not surprisingly, the list included bottled water and flashlights. More unexpected was the increase in sales of beer and strawberry Pop-Tarts.[15] In a more invasive example, Target created a "pregnancy prediction model" based on consumer purchases. A story in *The Power of Habit* by Charles Duhigg explains how the retailer used this model to predict that a teenager was pregnant and to send coupons to her home for pregnancy clothing and baby items, much to the surprise of her father.[16] Note here that careful analysis that led to insights is what makes this data useful to companies and advertisers.

The way data comes together with ad sales is this: using a cookie, a company tracks visitors to see who purchases its product and who doesn't. The company will then want to understand the common attributes of purchasers. The information the company collects for itself is called "first-party data." The company uses this information to find people similar to those who already purchase the product. So the company will execute what is known as "lookalike modeling," which means using data about existing consumers in order to

15. Constance L. Hays (November 14, 2004), "What Wal-Mart Knows About Customers' Habits," *New York Times*. Retrieved August 20, 2015 from http://www.nytimes.com/2004/11/14/business/your-money/14wal.html.

16. Charles Duhigg (February 16, 2012), "How Companies Learn Your Secrets," *The New York Times Magazine*. Retrieved September 13, 2015 from http://www.nytimes.com/2012/02/19/magazine/shopping-habits.html; Charles Duhigg, *The Power of Habit: Why We Do What We Do In Life And Business* (New York: Random House, 2012), 193.

find more like them. This is how a marketer described it to me: "So maybe out of 70,000 attributes, there were 250 that all of those people had in common . . . And the goal would be once you build those models, you facilitate those within the exchanges—hence the lookalike modeling—you wouldn't go out and target those people again, but you would go out into the wild of the exchanges and try to find people who had those 250 attributes of the customers you did get to convert."[17]

Alternatively, companies work with big data brokers, companies like BlueKai or Acxiom or Nielsen, to find new prospects. These companies have thousands of pieces of information on each person that they can provide to advertisers, known as "third-party data." Working with a data broker in this way is similar to traditional media methods: set behavioral parameters and target people who fit the behavior. Marketers combine first-party data and third-party data to target consumers no matter where they are online. They do this via an *advertising exchange*.

An ad exchange is like a stock exchange: it's a place where buyers (advertisers) and sellers (websites) connect to make a deal. You are not aware of this happening, but as you move around the web and you land on sites that are selling advertising through an exchange, millisecond auctions are being transacted in order to present an ad to you. It happens as the page is loading. If there is ad space available for real-time bidding, information about you and the page you're on is sent to an ad exchange.[18] In turn, the exchange asks advertisers to bid at auction. First- and third-party data are used to determine if the advertiser wants to bid. If the advertiser decides you are a good target for its product, the system needs to determine if

17. Interview with the author.
18. Christopher Ratcliff (2015, August 19), "A Super-Accessible Beginner's Guide to Programmatic Buying and RTB," *Econsultancy*. Retrieved September 2, 2015 from https://econsultancy.com/blog/65677-a-super-accessible-beginner-s-guide-to-programmatic-buying-and-rtb/.

there is a campaign that aligns with the information attached to the cookie. The exchange selects the winner from the many advertisers bidding and serves its ad to the website, and all this is done in milliseconds.

Data brokers are fundamental to this process. While old-time data companies had a few dozen piece of information on any one person, today's data brokers have hundreds and thousands of pieces of data. The biggest of these companies, Acxiom, claims to "execute more than 1 trillion global data transactions per week," has "multi-sourced insight into approximately 700 million consumers worldwide [and] demographics, life-stage segmentation, brand affinities, and purchase tendencies for nearly every adult consumer in the U.S."[19] This last translates to 1500 data points per American.[20] They and other brokers, like Corelogic, eBureau, ID Analytics, Intelius, and BlueKai, get this information from multiple sources: our "click stream," loyalty cards, the U.S. Post Office (which sells lists of when people move), public voting records, car registrations, and court filings (of bankruptcies),[21] among many others.[22] This information is used to segment us into behavioral categories, much like psychographics.[23] But because there is so much information that can be used to categorize people,

19. Acxiom Annual Report 2015, http://files.shareholder.com/downloads/ACXM/509790874x0x837305/D8BCBEA7-4C47-41CA-AB90-4AA58831CC53/Acxiom_Annual_Report_2015.pdf.
20. Katy Bachman (March 25, 2014), "Confessions of a Data Broker," *Adweek*. Retrieved August 18, 2015 from http://www.adweek.com/news/technology/confessions-data-broker-156437.
21. See PK List Marketing, Inc. http://www.pklistmarketing.com/index.htm.
22. Robert Scheer and Sara Beladi, *They Know Everything About You: How Data-Collecting Corporations and Snooping Government Agencies Are Destroying Democracy* (New York: Nation Books, 2015), p. 59.
23. See Nielsen for examples of psychographic segmentations: https://www.claritas.com/MyBestSegments/Default.jsp?ID=30&menuOption=segmentexplorer&pageName=Segment%2BExplorer#. Acxiom's categories are here: https://isapps.acxiom.com/personicx/personicx.aspx.

the segments are much more defined. Oracle (what used to be Datalogix), for example, has close to 2000 audience segments! Everything from car buyers (categorized as maximum spenders, car owners, and likely in the market to buy) to lifestyles (foodies, green consumers, sports fans). The "moms" segment alone has a dozen subgroups, from corporate moms to fit moms to stay-at-home moms.[24] Data brokers can also provide behavioral breakdowns based on shopping seasons. Acxiom, for example, segments back-to-school shoppers with groups like "Stylish Students," which might appeal to brands like H&M or Urban Outfitters; "Essential Electronics," for companies like Samsung and Apple; and even "The Early Bird," for customers who like to shop ahead of the crowd.[25] Marketers, and therefore data brokers, are particularly interested in people experiencing life changes like moving or having a baby because they spend more money on new items, from refrigerators to car seats. This explains why Target focused on expectant moms and why Experian, the credit report company, also has a marketing services division that maintains records of new and soon-to-be families.[26]

This is only the beginning. Big data will proliferate as we input more data into apps and FitBits and our Apple Watches. We cannot know what will be created as part of the Internet of Things, but we surely do know there will be advertising.

Doesn't this mean that the content no longer matters?

That's *exactly* what it means. If marketers can get inexpensive advertising online and they can directly target the individual based on behavior, the content itself becomes superfluous.

24. Oracle (n.d.), "The Audience Playbook," Retrieved November 21, 2016 from http://www.oracle.com/us/products/applications/audience-guide-3034880.pdf.
25. Acxiom (n.d.), "Data Packages." Retrieved September 15, 2015 from http://www.acxiom.com/data-packages/.
26. Ibid.

Are there other media that advertisers use in addition to television, print, and digital?

Advertising has become ubiquitous. No longer limited to media technology or billboards or buildings, advertising is on fruit, on cars, on bathroom stalls, in airports, on beaches and boardwalks, and in movie theaters. Out-of-home advertising used to be just billboards; now it is all of these and more. Just look around you. Where do you *not* see advertising?

What is product placement exactly and why is it so important to understand?

While there is the advertising you see, there is increasingly advertising you are less aware of. Called *native ads* and *content marketing*, these are forms of stealth marketing that we will cover at length in the following chapter. Their predecessor is product placement. Understanding the evolution of product placement helps to lay the groundwork for understanding the increasingly covert forms of advertising that exist online.

Product placement occurs when companies pay to have their product appear within a TV show, movie, videogame, music video, or a plethora of digital content. This is not new. Products were inserted into movies as early as the 1890s, but it didn't become standard practice until Steven Spielberg used Reese's Pieces to lure E.T. around the house—advertising that led to a 66 percent increase in sales.[27] Today, products are widely visible in films and the payments for their inclusion helps to offset the rising cost of movie production, which on average hovers around $100 million. Films themselves are forms of product placement, with the obvious example here being *The Lego Movie*, a film based on a long-beloved toy, which also included product plugs for the National Basketball

27. J.M. Lehu, *Branded Entertainment: Product Placement and Brand Strategy in the Entertainment Business* (London: Kogan Page, 2007).

Association and DC Comics, among others. There is even a documentary about the phenomenon called *The Greatest Movie Ever Sold*, produced by Morgan Spurlock, best known as the creator of *Super Size Me*. Payment for being included in these films is either in the form of cash or in-kind donations, such as Apple providing free iPhones and Airbooks to decorate a set.

Television has integrated products in a variety of ways throughout its history. As we saw, early on sponsors paid for the program and had their name attached to it. Product demonstrations or songs about the brand would be part of the flow of the show. More recently, product placement has been the purview of reality series. Most peg this to the launch of *Survivor*, as mentioned in Chapter 2. As we saw, instead of being separate, the products were embedded into the content. Other producers and advertisers quickly realized the value of this and products began to appear in any manner of contest-based reality series, from singing shows like *American Idol*, subtly (or not so subtly) selling Coca-Cola and Ford, to weight-loss contests like *The Biggest Loser* pushing an array of workout gadgets, to cooking shows hawking all sorts of food items. But it is not just reality series: *Modern Family*, *The Walking Dead*, and *Friday Night Lights* all push products from iPads to Hyundais. Talk shows give away retail gift cards, and Oprah gave cars to every member of her audience. Morning news shows are popular with advertisers because they allow for more fully fleshed-out segments that focus on the product. Gisele Bündchen did a two-minute segment on *Good Morning America* in conjunction with her Under Armour endorsement. We saw the same thing with the P&G "Thank You Mom" promotion for the Olympics. These have become staples of the programming—it provides content for the network and the brand gets an implied endorsement from the show's host. Online programming, like *Orange Is the New Black* and *House of Cards*, has followed suit and even pushed the limits.

The *Los Angeles Times* dubbed *House of Cards* the "house of product placement."[28] Advertisers pay for billboards in videogames, products are inserted into music videos, and even websites targeted to children contain commercial content. Beyond helping to offset production costs, the rise of product placement can be pegged to the introduction of Tivo and then the broad distribution of digital video recorders (DVRs). People were initially slow to see the value in this technology. While introduced in 2000, by 2007 only 17 percent of U.S. households had them. Network executives, however, were concerned early on about the device's ability to bypass commercials, particularly if DVRs gained wide acceptance. They were right to think so: today DVRs are in 48 percent of U.S. homes, and 60 percent of the users in those homes skip commercials.[29] The answer to this problem was to put the product into the program, where the message cannot be bypassed. In 2014, global spending on product placement was more than $10.5 billion, up 13.6 percent from the previous year.[30]

Do we perceive product placement the same way we look at commercials?

Yes and no. If you see a Coke can on a table, you are aware of its presence and it is likely to generate any thoughts and feelings

28. Matthew Fleischer (May 3, 2013), " 'House of Cards,' or More Like House Of Product Placement?" *Los Angeles Times*. Retrieved February 5, 2015 from http://articles.latimes.com/2013/may/03/entertainment/la-et-st-house-of-cards-netflix-product-placement-20130503.

29. PR Newswire (May 28, 2014), "2014 ARRIS Research Reveals Consumers Are Finding New Ways to Get Entertainment on Their Terms." Retrieved February 3, 2015 from http://ir.arrisi.com/mobile.view?c=87823&v=203&d=1&id=1935112.

30. PQ Media (March 13, 2015), "PQ Media: Double-Digit Surge in Product Placement Spend in 2014 Fuels Higher Global Branded Entertainment Growth As Media Integrations and Consumer Events Combo for $73.3B." Retrieved September 12, 2015 from http://www.prweb.com/releases/2015/02/prweb12487911.htm.

you might have about the brand, including, "Boy, that's really obvious product placement."

However, we approach programming differently than we do advertising. When we know we are looking at a sales pitch, we come with our critical wits intact. In contrast, we are more relaxed when watching a favorite TV show or a movie, so our defenses are down and we are more receptive to messages being presented. [31] In addition, we don't need to consciously engage with a product in order for our attitudes about the brand to be influenced.[32] Here's the difference: if you see ABC Sports using GoPro cameras, you might think, "If ABC Sports uses these, they must be really good." If you see an ad for GoPro cameras, you are more likely to think, "That looks like a great camera, but I wonder what it costs."

How does product placement work online?

Since content online is different, product placement has morphed to fit the format. Instead of characters using an iPhone within the context of a TV show, we see our favorite celebrities wearing the latest, greatest $600 headphones on Instagram, Facebook, and Twitter. Within this environment, we are less likely to think of this as an endorsement, even though the celebrity was paid, either in cash or in kind, to wear the product. This practice is not new; it is what PR people have done for decades. What is new is marrying celebrities to products and the ability to generate a significant number of media impressions. In one example, a PR company working for Bang & Olufsen headphones generated a total of 570 million

31. "Movies May Carry a Hidden Pitch." (n.d.), *The Free Library*. Retrieved September 8, 2015 from http://www.thefreelibrary.com/Movies+May+Carry+a+Hidden+Pitch.-a058037919.
32. Lehu, *Branded Entertainment*, 2000, p. 63; Robert B. Zajonc (1968), "Attitudinal Effects of Mere Exposure," *Journal of Personality and Social Psychology* 9(2, pt. 2): 1–27.

impressions through a combination of "likes" as well as press and online impressions.[33]

Product placement gets a bit more complex on social media sites like Facebook. Here, the goal is to have you "like" a lot of products and a lot of celebrities. Then, when a celebrity "likes" a product because he or she has been paid to do so, it generates a triangle of engagement: you–the celebrity–the brand. The best part is that the marketer can determine what celebrities to associate with its brand and can track your brand interactions. So, for example, if you are a fan of Lady Gaga and she "likes" MAC cosmetics, and then you "like" Lady Gaga and MAC, then this becomes a dual endorsement to your friends; you become the means to sell MAC products to your friends. Thus, unwittingly, you become part of the marketing. Clicking "like" buttons, then, is not about demonstrating your interest but about creating newfangled product placement.

The advantages of product placement online are easy to see. For marketers, it is much easier to track product placement online because the information can be sent directly to their computer systems. With television, trying to put a value figure on this strategy was almost impossible. Marketers can also track which advertising method is most effective. So if you see your favorite celebrity wearing really cool headphones on Facebook, you simply have to click to buy; at the same time, the marketer can know what motivated you to do so.

So if digital advertising, and particularly product seeding, is so effective, why do advertisers still use other media?

Because 92 percent of retail sales happen offline.[34] Also, while we spend a lot of time online, we spend much more time in the real world . . . at least I hope we do.

33. KPFR, "Bang & Olufsen Luxury Headphones." Retrieved June 15, 2015 from http://kfpr.tv/product-seeding.
34. Greg Sterling (June 15, 2016), "Why Location Is the Hottest Topic in Digital Marketing Right Now," *MarketingLand*. Retrieved November 21,

Can we expect advertising to continue to be wherever the eye can see?

Yes. As noted, capitalism is based on growth. Every quarter, corporations have to announce their earnings to Wall Street, and the perpetual need to increase sales means a ratcheting up of the marketing that supports it.

At the same time, competition is increasing in almost any product category you can think of. Simply look at the shelves of your local supermarket. The average number of items in a store in 2014 was 42,214 versus 15,000 in 1980.[35] Each of those items means more communications clutter—not only within media formats but everywhere the eye can see. To "break through the clutter," advertisers turn to more outrageous communication to get your attention—more intrusion, more sex, and more vulgarity.

And if making more noise doesn't lead to more sales, then new markets need to be found. This has led to advertisers targeting younger and younger audiences. It has also led to marketers pushing products overseas that they can't sell in the United States; cigarettes are a good example of this.

As long as growth remains the goal, we can expect this trend to continue, and with it the incumbent issues of noise pollution and environmental degradation will continue.

2016 from http://marketingland.com/location-hottest-topic-digital-marketing-right-now-181059.

35. Food Marketing Institute, "Supermarket Facts." Retrieved November 21, 2016 from http://www.fmi.org/research-resources/supermarket-facts; Marion Nestle, *Food Politics: How the Food Industry Influences Nutrition and Health* (Berkeley: University of California Press, 2013). Retrieved May 25, 2016 from http://www.findarticles.com/p/articles/mi_m0813/is_7_29/ai_90980246.

7

ADVERTISING
IN THE DIGITAL AGE

How come ads seem to follow me around the Internet?

This is what is known as *retargeting*. Remember we talked about
the sales funnel? In that paradigm, marketers want to interact
with you as far down the funnel as possible, the best place being
the point of sale. Online, that means the shopping cart. If you put
an item into the cart—say, a pair of jeans or the latest bestseller—
and then decide you don't have time to buy it right away, an ad
for that product will begin to follow you around the Internet. And
it will go from your computer to your cellphone to your iPad or
other tablet. The same holds true if you are doing research for
something to buy. You begin looking into vacations on Cape Cod
or a bicycle trip to Ireland and you can be sure that competitive
advertising will follow—even after you book your trip.

And how can ads follow me from one device to another?

Marketers had been concerned up until recently about how to
follow us on mobile devices rather than our computers. This
was an issue because cookies work on our laptops but have
limited functionality on mobile devices. Moreover, they vary
in terms of their usefulness in apps versus the mobile web as
well as across devices.[1] One limitation, for example, is that

1. IAB (n.d.), "Understanding Mobile Cookies." Retrieved September 3,
   2015 from http://www.iab.net/media/file/IABDigitalSimplified-
   MobileCookies.pdf.

cookies are unique to individual apps, thus limiting their ability to be shared with other apps and mobile web browsers.

Marketers had to find a way to work around these limitations. According to Arvind Narayanan, a professor of computer science at Princeton, "Let's say you have a laptop and a smartphone, and you're traveling with them, and you're browsing the web through Wi-Fi ... The advertiser, or other company, notices that there are two particular devices that always connect to the website from the same network. The chance of this happening coincidentally is similar to the chance of two people having the same travel itinerary, so, after a period of time, if it keeps happening, they can deduce that it's the same person that owns those two different devices. Now they can put your browsing behavior on one device together with your browsing behavior on the other device and use it to build a deeper profile."[2] New proprietary technologies developed by companies such as drawbrig.ge and Tapad can seamlessly track us across devices. From Tapad's website: "Our Device Graph Technology combines proprietary, first party, and third party data to anonymously identify an individual. So whether they're at the office on their desktop, watching a show on their connected TV, or traveling to another city with their smartphone, you can hone your content delivery to the right audience."[3]

Another method that marketers have used to improve the value of apps is to integrate the online and offline worlds, so-called augmented reality. We are talking here, of course, about Pokémon GO. In the summer of 2016, this gaming app became an overnight sensation, increasing the company's value by $9 billion in two days—that's right, two days—and

2. Simon Hill (June 27, 2015), "How Much Do Online Advertisers Really Know about You? We Asked an Expert," *Digital Trends.* Retrieved August 30, 2015 from http://www.digitaltrends.com/ computing/how-do-advertisers-track-you-online-we-found-out/ #ixzz3hi6O5qmF.
3. See Tapad at http://www.tapad.com/lifestyle/advertising.

users spent more time with the app than users of WhatsApp, Instagram, Snapchat, and Messenger.[4] While users—kids, teens, and adults alike—saw the app as free and fun and a way to get outside, what they did not see was all the marketing attached. Initially, this was in the form of data collection. Clicking the legal agreement for the app gave Niantic, the producer of the app, permission to access personal information like your contacts and your location. Niantic also received permission to share that information with other companies. Fifteen million people downloaded the app, so we're talking about a lot of data—and a lot of that data is about kids. So it surprised almost no one that the company used McDonald's as PokeStops and Pokémon Gyms—places players had to visit in the real world to play the game. This was no coincidence: it is a paid sponsorship. So much in the same way that the Internet has turned your computer into a shopping mall, so too Niantic has turned gaming into a shopping trip. On the plus side, the app has been very good for small local businesses who can inexpensively lure customers to their retail stores.

When I am being tracked, do marketers really know that it is me by name?

Marketers claim they do not know who is connected to an IP address, nor do they care—at least not beyond the behavior that occurs on the computer, particularly as it relates to product purchases.

While this rings true and, from my discussions with people in the industry, I think it is, this does not mean that the information connected to our computer is anonymous. A number of books, and certainly Edward Snowden, have proved this point.

4. Trey Williams (July 12, 2016), "How Pokémon Go Makes Money," *MarketWatch*. Retrieved August 18, 2016 from http://www.marketwatch.com/story/how-pokemon-go-makes-money-2016-07-11.

Two *New York Times* reporters were able identify a sixty-two-year-old Georgia woman using anonymous search data from AOL. University of Texas researchers have "de-anonymized" information from Netflix's database, including information about political preferences. One particularly concerning fact from Julia Angwin's book *Dragnet Nation* is that "75 percent of the top one thousand websites included code from social networks that could match people's names with their Web-browsing habits." What this means is that if you don't sign out of Facebook, whenever you are on a site that has the "like" button, Facebook can track you to the site—even if you don't click the button. This holds true for other social sites as well. Speaking of "likes," researchers analyzed those seemingly innocuous "likes" of 58,466 Americans and were able to accurately "predict a range of highly sensitive personal attributes including: sexual orientation, ethnicity, religious and political views, personality traits, intelligence, happiness, use of addictive substances, parental separation, age, and gender."[5]

This is not to scare you, but to make you aware. Every click is tracked. Every post is noted, even to the point of knowing when you have edited your ideas. Companies know what, where, and how we search. They know how long we spend on a page, a site, and where we move to when we're done. In addition to tracking our moves, companies experiment with what we do online. One example is the A/B testing of advertising. It can be more personal than this, however. In one example, online dating site OkCupid manipulated data to lead people to believe they were a good match when they weren't. Given this wrong information, people "liked" the mismatches. This is a well-known type of experiment called *priming*. It is rarely used in this way to play with emotions. In a true research setting, an

5. Michal Kosinski, David Stillwell, and Thore Graepel (April 9, 2013), "Private Traits and Attributes Are Predictable from Digital Records of Human Behavior," *Proceedings of the National Academy of Sciences of the United States.* Retrieved September 13, 2015 from http://www.pnas.org/content/110/15/5802.full.

experiment like this wouldn't be allowed. Online, though, we are fair game. As Christian Rudder, OkCupid's founder, put it: "Guess what, everybody: if you use the Internet, you're the subject of hundreds of experiments at any given time, on every site. That's how websites work."[6] Truer words were never said. Unfortunately, none of this is done for our benefit. The data and the research and the emotional manipulation are all in the name of selling more products—most of which we probably don't even need.

Can advertisers connect my online activity with what I do in the real world?

Yes. This is called *onboarding*.

The connection is made through your email address. When the salespeople at your local Bath & Body Works or Banana Republic ask for your email so they can send you information about discounts and special sales, what they are really doing is trying to get access to your email so they can connect online and offline consumer behavior. This is how it works: the store shares your email address with an onboarding company like LiveRamp, which is owned by big data firm Acxiom. You sign in to websites online using your email address. If those sites are ones the onboarding company does business with, the company can connect your online activity to your device and your name.[7]

6. Charlie Warzel (July 28, 2014), "OkCupid Data Scientist: 'I'm Not Playing God'," BuzzFeed. Retrieved July 14, 2015 from http://www.buzzfeed.com/charliewarzel/ok-cupid-data-scientist-im-not-playing-god.
7. Simon Hill (June 27, 2015), "How Much Do Online Advertisers Really Know about You? We Asked An Expert," *Digital Trends*. Retrieved August 30, 2015 from http://www.digitaltrends.com/computing/how-do-advertisers-track-you-online-we-found-out/#ixzz3hi6O5qmF.

What are the other issues associated with big data?

In addition to privacy and surveillance, there is the issue of accuracy. The more data collected, the more chance to get it wrong. You can check out some of the data Acxiom has on you at aboutthedata.com. I say "some" because what the company allows you to see is limited. What I saw about myself was more or less accurate, though according to the Acxiom data I was still married even though I had been divorced for ten years—a fact that should have be easily entered into the database.

Most disturbing is the level to which data mining is used against us. Decisions are made based not only on what we post, but also on what friends post, which is something we have no control over.[8] If a number of your friends on Facebook are in the military, then the U.S. Army is going to be apt to recruit you. If you are a Mac user, you may have been shown more expensive hotel options by Orbitz because of your discerning character.[9] There is also something called *dynamic pricing*, a tactic used by retailers like Staples and Home Depot, whereby products are priced differently based on where you live (geolocation) and how you shop online.[10] Far worse are financial institutions that reject loan applications based on someone's social network. The lending institution is making an assumption that if your friend is a deadbeat then you are likely to be one, too. Facebook allows these practices, what we

8. Adam Tanner. *What Stays in Vegas: The World of Personal Data— Lifeblood Of Big Business—And The End Of Privacy As We Know It* (New York: PublicAffairs, 2014), p. 101.
9. Dana Mattioli (August 23, 2012), "On Orbitz, Mac Users Steered to Pricier Hotels," *Wall Street Journal*. Retrieved September 5, 2015 from http://www.wsj.com/articles/SB10001424052702304458604577488822667325882.
10. Thorin Klosowski (January 7, 2013), "How Web Sites Vary Prices Based on Your Information (and What You Can Do About It)," *Lifehacker*. Retrieved September 5, 2015 from http://lifehacker.com/5973689/how-web-sites-vary-prices-based-on-your-information-and-what-you-can-do-about-it; Eli Pariser, *The Filter Bubble: What the Internet is Hiding from You* (New York: Penguin, 2011).

called *redlining* in the real world, which typically discriminate based on race.[11]

University of Maryland law professor Frank Pasquale calls the misuse of information "runaway data." Others have dubbed it "big data hubris." Whatever term we use, the bottom line is that as we are surrounded by more data, we assume that in and of itself it is useful, but that is simply not the case. As noted earlier, it is not the data but the data analysis that makes the difference. Google Flu is an example of such hubris. Google claimed it could track influenza faster than the U.S. Centers for Disease Control and Prevention because people with the flu look up ways to relieve their symptoms. Turns out this didn't work as planned because people typed in "flu" without having a clear diagnosis. Score for Google Flu: wrong 100 out of 108 weeks.[12]

To assuage us, companies explain why a particular ad was sent to us. Facebook does this with a video, as do traditional publishers, many of whom will then send you to the Digital Advertising Alliance (http://www.aboutads.info/).[13] Here, the story is framed as big data working to serve us "better ads." Perhaps some data could do that, but do companies really need to have thousands of pieces of information on us? And do marketers need all the information that is being collected? One marketer I spoke to said all he really wanted to know was how people found his site, how long they stayed, what they

11. Mark Sullivan (August 4, 2015), "Facebook Patents Technology To Help Lenders Discriminate against Borrowers Based on Social Connections," *Venture Beat*. Retrieved August 5, 2015 from http://venturebeat.com/2015/08/04/facebook-patents-technology-to-help-lenders-discriminate-against-borrowers-based-on-social-connections/.
12. David Lazer, Ryan Kennedy, Gary King, and Alessandro Vespignani (March 14, 2014), "The Parable of Google Flu: Traps in Big Data Analysis," *Science* 343 (6176):1203–1205.
13. About Facebook ads: https://www.facebook.com/help/585318558251813. About Cosmopolitan ads: http://www.cosmopolitan.com/about/oba-policy.

did on his site, and where they went when they left. Which begs the question: Why collect so much data? In part, marketers use it to justify their jobs. Since what they do is tracked and quantified, not only do they have to demonstrate sales (which is no longer the sole metric for success) but they also have to create key performance indicators (KPIs), which are methods of assessing return on investment (ROI) such as establishing relationships with consumers through social media.

No one ever asked if we wanted to be tracked. Eighty-two percent of global consumers claim that companies are gathering too much data about us.[14] We're not willing to give our information away for free, even if it means we don't have to pay for Facebook and Google.[15] No one ever asked if we wanted every story about our lives to be forever available on the Internet, even after we may have moved on to be better, more productive, and simply more private people. While little has been done about this in the United States, either by the Federal Trade Commission or the government, in Western Europe it is a different story. There, "right to be forgotten laws" require "all data collectors to provide individuals with access to their data, the ability to correct errors in that data, and, in some cases, the right to delete the data."[16] Imagine if you could ask a corporation to delete unflattering material about you and it had to comply: oh, what a different place Facebook would be!

14. *Trendwatching* (January 2014), "7 Consumer Trends to Run with in 2014." Retrieved March 7, 2015 from http://trendwatching.com/trends/7trends2014/#no-data.
15. Joseph Turow, Michael Hennessy, and Nora Draper (2015), "The Tradeoff Fallacy: How Marketers Are Misrepresenting American Consumers and Opening Them Up to Exploitation," Annenberg School for Communication, University of Pennsylvania. Retrieved October 1, 2015 from https://www.asc.upenn.edu/sites/default/files/TradeoffFallacy_1.pdf.
16. Julia Angwin, *Dragnet Nation: A Quest for Privacy, Security, and Freedom in a World of Relentless Surveillance* (New York: Times Books, 2014), p. 86.

Is there a way to stop marketers from tracking me?

On your computer, the best thing to do is to clear out your cookies every day. If you don't, the information will stay attached to the cookies for 3 months. You can also stop using your phone for anything except phone calls (I realize that's probably hard to imagine).

What are ad blockers?

Ad blockers can help you from being tracked both online and on your mobile device. Adblocker Plus is one of the most popular products. However, an increasing number of sites will not allow you to view their content if you are using an ad blocking extension.

Whether you choose to use the technology to block ads or not, it is useful to see how and how many companies, like data brokers and ad exchanges, are attempting to gain access to your computer. Two that I find helpful are Ghostery and Disconnect. When you put these extensions on your browser, they will enable you to see how many organizations are accessing your computer by listing them as the website populates. With that information, you can decide which sites you want to interact with. One site I visited listed more than 6000 companies trying to access my computer; I did not go back to that site again. As well as listing companies such as DoubleClick (an ad network owned by Google), big data firms like AddThis, and ad exchanges like BrightRoll, Disconnect gives you the option of presenting the data as an infographic. In the middle of the illustration is a circle representing the site you are on, and coming off that circle are spokes that have circles on the end that contain the name of the company tracking you. Seeing dozens of bubbles floating on the screen gives you a visceral sense of just have surveilled you are.

However, even ad blockers are turning out to be not all they were cracked up to be. In September 2016, AdBlocker Plus announced that it would begin selling "acceptable" ads.[17]

What is stealth marketing and why has it proliferated?

Stealth marketing is defined as "the use of surreptitious marketing practices that fail to disclose or reveal the true relationship with the company that produces or sponsors the marketing message."[18] This is not new. Product placement was an early form of stealth marketing, but with the introduction of social media, hidden marketing practices are more widespread and more obscure. The most widely used forms of stealth marketing today are native advertising and content marketing.

Advertisers have had to make their messages covert because we have become so adept at avoiding advertising, first with DVRs that allowed us to skip ads, then streaming series that don't contain advertising, and now using ad blockers. All of these practices explain why advertisers seek to make their messages blend in to the surrounding content.

What is native advertising?

Native advertising, as the name suggests, is advertising that is created to feel indigenous to the site on which it appears.

The Internet Advertising Bureau (IAB) has established that there are six types of native advertising: paid search units, recommendation widgets, promoted listings, in-feed units, in-ad

17. Olivia Solon (2016, September 13), "Adblock Plus Launching Platform to Sell 'Acceptable' Ads," *The Guardian*. Retrieved November 21, 2016 from https://www.theguardian.com/business/2016/sep/13/adblock-plus-launching-platform-to-sell-acceptable-ads.
18. Kelly D. Martin and N. Craig Smith (February 2008), "Commercializing Social Interaction: The Ethics of Stealth Marketing," INSEAD Business School Research Paper No. 2008/19/ISIC. Available at *SSRN*: http://ssrn.com/abstract=1111976; Rob Walker, *Buying In: What We Buy and Who We Are* (New York: Random House, 2010).

with native element units and custom (or "can't be contained") formats. Paid search units are the ads you see at the top of search engines, like Google or Bing. They look like a response to a query but they have a small box next to them that says "ad" just before the link to the site. Recommendation widgets are the suggestions for content that appear on the bottom of a webpage. You might be reading a story on an app or a news site and at the bottom there will be a list of "recommended stories," or articles listed under the line "from around the web." These are ads distributed by companies like Outbrain, Sharethrough, and Taboola.

The most common forms of native advertising are in-feed ads and custom formats. In-feed native ads appear in social media feeds and within newsfeeds. Custom ads are individually created (i.e., customized for each advertiser) and are typically produced by the publisher in order to ensure the advertising looks and feels like the noncommercial content.

Can you give some examples of in-feed ads?

On Facebook native ads look like anything else in your newsfeed. The distinction, however, is that native ads have not been sent by a friend (well, mostly) but by an advertiser. They have the name of the advertiser where your friend's name would be and the time stamp under their name is replaced with the word "sponsor" in very light gray type. The placement and the subtlety of the commercial designation are done on purpose: advertisers want you to engage with this information the same way you would with a post from a friend. Another version of native ads in this format are the ones that say, "Susie Smith, John Jones and Amy Brown like XYZ Company."

Native ads are similarly presented on Instagram (owned by Facebook), Twitter, and other social media. They all have some labeling designating that they are advertising, but much of this is so small or so obscured as to be almost invisible. Also, the language denoting the ads can be confusing because there is no uniformity. Sites use everything from "advertisement" or "ad" to "promoted" or "promoted by" to "sponsored post," "pre-sented by [XYZ Company]" and, most confusing, "Featured Partner."

In-feed ads are not only on social media but ubiquitous, appearing in news sites including Business Insider, Talking Points Memo (TPM), FastCompany, Mashable, Gawker, Salon, Slate, and Vox, as well as in music sites like iHeartMedia and Pandora.

The most widely used form of native advertising is called *endemic in-feed units*, which are typically written by a market-ing unit within the publication so that it fully replicates the voice and appearance of the site. The company most known for this type of native advertising is BuzzFeed. As you likely know, BuzzFeed is a website mostly known for quizzes like "What Shoe Is Your Solemate," listicles like "15 Toys From Our Childhood That Were Way Too Good To Share," and just about anything to do with kittens. Whether listicle or quiz, it may be an ad or not, and most times it is difficult to tell one way or the other. The two examples here were actually ads for Famous Footwear and Taco Bell. Similar to the in-feed ads, there is sponsorship denoted at the beginning of the post, but little is done to draw attention to it. What initially differentiated BuzzFeed from the competition is that BuzzFeed works with the client to produce the advertising so that it will seamlessly work within the content. One of its most successful ventures was with Purina and a video called "Dear Kitten." The piece is incredibly entertaining and has had a series of spinoff ads. Advertising that is so entertaining you will watch it anyway is the very *raison d'être* of native ads. You don't mind so much seeing the can of Purina cat food when it is wrapped in a two-minute video that makes you laugh.

Native appears on mobile platforms as well and can be very deceptive. The dating app Tinder, for example, is widely popu-lar with millennials, so it is a go-to advertising vehicle for mar-keters. Men at the ultra-hip SXSW festival were matched with Ava, a stunning 25-year-old woman. As is the case with these types of apps, the conversation moves from banter to where to meet. "If you could meet me anywhere, where would you choose?" asks Ava. "Considering we're both in Austin right now, I'd have to say Austin," is the man's response. "You are clever," says Ava. "You've passed my test. Take a look at my Instagram, and let me know if I've passed yours:). @meetava." Once there, the prospective date learns that Ava is no woman; she's a robot, and the Instagram account was for a film called *Ex Machina*. Deceptive and manipulative promotions like these are sure to increase as publishers move content to mobile devices.

Who uses custom native advertising and what does it look like?

Custom native is being used by news and entertainment sites, and it is content that is very difficult to separate from the editorial. It is specially produced by the publisher so it looks like the rest of the website. Unlike BuzzFeed, which also produces customized content, this is not created to appear within a newsfeed.

Almost every major newspaper uses custom content, notably the *New York Times*, the *Washington Post*, and the *Wall Street Journal*. The *Times*'s first native ad was a piece about women in prison. It looked like any other article that might appear in the paper. There was a headline, "Women Inmates: Why the Male Model Doesn't Work," and a byline of the "reporter." There was a graphic of women entering a prison and there were a number of videos. But this wasn't unbiased *Times* journalism. It was an ad paid for by Netflix as a promotion for its series *Orange Is the New Black*. This material was produced by the newspaper's in-house marketing arm called T Brand Studio, which is staffed with people who have considerable journalistic and marketing credentials. This piece is not like what appears on BuzzFeed, however, because it is in-depth reporting. The question is, though, is it news? Since the initial foray into this type of advertising, the *Times* has moved into this area apace, creating specialized content for big-name advertisers like GE, Ford, and Google. Some content, though, is questionable from an ethical perspective. For example, early on there was a piece paid for by Goldman Sachs that was an obvious attempt to make them look better in the midst of the Great Recession. A more recent piece called "College is still worth it, despite rising costs" was paid for by Discover Student Loans, a division of Discover cards and a vastly more expensive lending option than others available to students and their families.[19]

The first newspaper to produce custom native was the *Washington Post*, which is owned by Amazon's Jeff Bezos. Beginning in 2013, the paper allowed posts on its home page. The *Post* also has a space in its opinion section, called "BrandConnect Perspective," where companies can submit pieces written by corporate executives. Like the *New York Times*, the *Post* has an in-house studio, which is called BrandConnect. According to *Adweek*, this team "sits in the marketing group but looks for inspiration in the newsroom."[20] The *Wall Street Journal* came on board with its WSJ Custom Studios a year later. As a financial newspaper, the *Journal* provides not only news-like pieces with infographics but also research and white papers. As with the *Times*, Netflix used native advertising, but this time it was to promote its series *Narco*. The *Journal* created an elaborate website that opens with a black screen. On it is red type reading "The Story behind the Medellín Cartel," which stays on the screen while the site downloads. Once loaded, the screen is black with the word "Cocainenomics" written in lines of white powder. When the visitor scrolls down, there are stories with bylines, interactive maps, and video.

Beyond newspapers, any number of entertainment sites are also using custom native. Traditional media properties like

19. See T Brand Studio at http://www.tbrandstudio.com/our-work/.
20. Lucia Moses (March 3, 2014), "The Washington Post's Native Ads Get Editorial Treatment," *Adweek*. Retrieved May 10, 2015 from http://www.adweek.com/news/press/washington-posts-native-ads-get-editorial-treatment-156048.

CBS Interactive and Condé Nast, for example, are offering this marketing format. With Condé Nast—publisher of magazines like *GQ*, *Vanity Fair*, and *The New Yorker*, among many others— there isn't any pretense of separating content from advertising, as the publisher readily has advertisers work with its editorial staff through its in-house studio, called "23 Stories by Condé Nast." In part, this may come from experience with the magazine *Vogue*, which people read as much for the ads as for the articles.[21]

As for cutting-edge media, millennial-favorite VICE readily uses native, and unlike other sites it does very little to alert the reader to the sponsored content. The same holds true for fashion and style site Refinery29. This site, which has been around since 2005, covers runway trends and offers beauty tips as well as world news and soft news and has attracted such significant audiences that it is often compared with *Vogue* and *InStyle*. Notes one industry insider, "Their content is excellent. Sometimes, it's hard to distinguish between Refinery29's editorial content and its branded content, meaning that they're both equally engaging."[22]

But aren't native ads obvious?

No, actually. In research done by scholars from the University of Georgia, only 8 percent of people are able to recognize native

21. Steven Perlberg (January 26, 2015), "Condé Nast Unveils Branded Content Shop Powered By Editors," *CMO Today*. Retrieved June 20, 2015 from http://blogs.wsj.com/cmo/2015/01/26/23-stories-conde-nast-branded-content/.
22. Ann Gynn (July 17, 2015), "Content Marketing Experts Reveal Which Brands Are Pushing the Envelope," *Content Marketing Institute*. Retrieved August 20, 2015 from http://contentmarketinginstitute.com/2015/07/experts-brands-pushing-envelope/?utm_medium=email&utm_source=Act-On+Software&utm_content=email&utm_campaign=Content%20Marketing%20Experts%20Reveal%20Which%20Brands%20are%20Pushing%20the%20Envelope&utm_term=READ%20THIS%20ARTICLE.

ads.[23] Or, if we look at Google, the largest recipient of digital advertising spending, the confusion exists even after a decade of paid search—41 percent of visitors to the site could not tell the difference between paid search and organic listings.[24]

So how can we know that an article or video is advertising?

There is no guarantee, but once you know what to look for it can begin to become more obvious.

For in-feed ads, look for anything that says "sponsored" or "promoted by" or "featured partner." Particularly look at the top of the webpage or the mobile app. On the *New York Times*, there is a light blue bar saying "PAID POST" that runs across the top of the page. Also, the URL for a native ad begins with paidpost.nytimes.com.

Bear in mind, however, that the point of these ads is for you *not* to recognize them so that you will be willing to spend more time with them and will be more willing to pass them on to others. Advertisers are looking for the patina of a major newspaper to rub off on their brand, and while the newspapers claim not to be hiding anything, it is hard to believe that, given the lengths they go to make the content look so indigenous. Fairness and Accuracy in Reporting (FAIR)'s Janine Jackson, who believes they are being disingenuous at best, says, "Native, shnative. The *New York Times* should not be in the business of managing people's opinion of Goldman Sachs. There is no way that I can take as seriously the *New York Times*

23. Bartosz W. Wojdynski and Nathaniel J. Evans (2016), "Going Native: Effects of Disclosure Position and Language on the Recognition and Evaluation of Online Native Advertising," *Journal of Advertising* 45(2): 157–168.
24. Graham Charlton (February 28, 2013), "40% of Consumers Are Unaware That Google Adwords are Adverts," *Econsultancy.com*. Retrieved August 18, 2015 from https://econsultancy.com/blog/62249-40-of-consumers-are-unaware-that-google-adwords-are-adverts#i.1iuztbw1504fas.

reporting on Goldman Sachs knowing that they have just been on this content creation journey together. It very simply represents another example of news outlets doing pretty much the definition of 'selling out.' Native advertising is just an effort to confuse readers to think that they're getting something other than an ad."[25]

How pervasive is native advertising?

Estimates are that close to 90 percent of online publishers are using some form of native ads.[26] In terms of dollar figures, native advertising was close to $8 billion in 2015 and is expected to reach $21 billion by 2018, according to Business Insider and the Interactive Advertising Bureau (IAB).[27]

Are there any regulations for native advertising?

No. For the most part, the industry regulates itself.

In December 2015, the Federal Trade Commission issued guidelines for native advertising. These called for uniform labeling. The IAB called these guidelines "overly prescriptive," suggesting that advertisers and publishers do not want to make these ads readily discernible.

25. Will Yong (April 12, 2015), "The Rise of Native Advertising In The News Media," *Al Jazeera*. Flash video. Retrieved June 10, 2015 from http://www.aljazeera.com/programmes/listeningpost/2015/04/native-advertising-trust-sale-150411130613310.html.
26. *eMarketer* (n.a.) (July 22, 2013), "How Native Ad Campaigns Are Shaping Up: Definitions of Native Advertising Still Vary." Retrieved June 10, 2015 from http://www.emarketer.com/Article/How-Native-Ad-Campaigns-Shaping-Up/1010064.
27. Mark Hoelzel (May 20, 2015), "Spending on Native Advertising is Soaring as Marketers and Digital Media Publishers Realize the Benefits," *Business Insider*. Retrieved May 21, 2015 from http://www.businessinsider.com/spending-on-native-ads-will-soar-as-publishers-and-advertisers-take-notice-2014-11.

What is the difference between native ads
and content marketing?

Native advertising are ads that are made to look like the website on which they appear. Content marketing is content—an article or more likely a video—that has been produced by a marketing company but has little to no branding in it. The content is meant to be informative or entertaining to the members of a specific target audience without hitting them on the head with a sales message, and the content appears on a site owned by the marketers, either a website, a blog, or even their Facebook or Instagram page. One marketer explained it to me this way: "Content marketing is much longer term [than native advertising]. When it's done right, it should be completely devoid of solicitation. It's about adding value and giving, not receiving. The strategy is 'I'm going to keep adding value to your life and proving that I'm an expert on this topic that you care about, and when it comes time for you to buy and you decide that you need something we might have, hopefully we'll be top of mind.'" Importantly, then, content marketing occurs over a sustained time period and is not intrusive.

The goal of content marketing is to create a relationship with consumers by providing them with useful information. Then, when they get to the point when they are ready to buy, they will think about the marketer's product. This content exists on owned media, like blogs or magazines, and tends to be viewed by being distributed through social media. Social media sites also act as owned content. YouTube channels or Instagram pages are forms of owned media.

Some content marketing can be quite elaborate. Intel created four film series that appeared online with incredibly high production values and elaborate social media engagement. The first three series were done in conjunction with Toshiba. The first ran in the summer of 2011 and was called "Inside," which is a running theme and marries up with the brand's tagline, which has been variously been "Intel Inside," "Look

Inside," and, more recently, "Experience What's Inside." In this mystery, a girl is trapped in a room with a Toshiba computer. The marketer supplied clues on Facebook and Twitter to help people solve the whodunit. A more intricate campaign came the following year with a series called "The Beauty Inside." The story was based on a man named Alex who wakes up every day to find out he is someone else; he is the same inside but different outside. The brilliant twist was that fans auditioned to play Alex via Facebook, and ultimately more than 70 people were integrated into the films. "The Power Inside," the third series, starred Harvey Keitel and included an online audition element. The most recent Intel series, "What Lives Inside," is the most ambitious in terms of production values. It was directed by Oscar winner Robert Stromberg and starred a major lineup of talent, including Catherine O'Hara, Colin Hanks (son of Tom Hanks), and Oscar winner J.K. Simmons. The film looks like a Tim Burton movie and is the story of creative self-discovery. Hanks, who begins the film in a gray, boring job, comes to find his artistic talent. And this time, instead of including people, the film included their artwork, which had been submitted via social media.

I spent some extra time explaining this because it illustrates how content marketing works. The content is beautiful and entertaining in a way that a commercial about a computer processor cannot be. Yet it communicates the core brand message, the importance of what is inside, and it does so in a way that will appeal to the millennial target audience, who tends to be jaded toward traditional marketing methods. The goal, according to Billie Goldman of Intel and Josh Brandau of ad agency Pereira & O'Dell, was to reach 18- to 34-year-olds and to "deliver an unexpected experience that exceeded their expectations and drove an emotional connection for the Intel and Toshiba brands." Intel was irrelevant to this target audience; Toshiba was a brand their fathers would use. To change this perception, they turned the product into a "character in the film" while integrating consumers so that the story was "as much about the audience as it was about the brands."[28] The series has run for several years to build interest and interconnection between the brands and prospective consumers. None of this is being done by screaming at consumers to buy, buy, buy. Instead, the marketer is asking consumers to spend time with its message in the hopes that they will find it engaging enough to share it with others.

Remember that content marketing is about the marketer creating its own content for its own media spaces. While Intel created a site called Insidefilms.com that houses the videos, Coca-Cola revamped its corporate website to be a digital magazine and called the site "Coca-Cola's Journey." The tagline is "Refreshing the world, one story at a time," good evidence that Coke is pursuing a content marketing strategy. The site is obviously that of Coca-Cola. But remember, whether it has to do with this site or BuzzFeed, most people interact with the content on social media, so some of the brand indicators are going to be less evident. This is key because "about 60 percent of Journey's content has a connection to the company or brand. The rest—pieces on music, style, innovation, careers, and sports—aligns with the company's values." These include everything from food and travel to career and culture, all with varying levels of connection to the brand.

Another example of a site providing content in this manner is one that you likely have not heard of. Van Winkle's is a digital magazine about sleep. It has news stories about posttraumatic stress disorder and sleep disorders and stories on topics like jet lag; it even did a story about Michelle Obama having the Girls Scouts come to the White House for a sleepover. In the product section, there are articles about the reading app Oyster and fitness trackers. Like the native ads for the *New York Times*,

28. Billie Goldman and Josh Brandau (October 20–23, 2013), "The Next Wave of Digital Marketing," slide presentation for iMedia conference in Austin, Texas. Retrieved June 30, 2015 from http://www.slideshare. net/imediaconnection/2013-10breakthroughintelpereira-odell.

the content is written by award-winning journalists. This is no simple sleep website, however: this is an ad for Casper, a mattress company that sells directly to consumers, much the same way as socially conscious eyewear company Warby Parker cut out the middle man.

Another popular form of content marketing is web series. Chipotle had a series on Hulu called "Farmed and Dangerous." Like "Back to the Farm" and "Scarecrow," this series highlighted the negative aspects of processed food while promoting the sponsor as a sustainable and healthy alternative. Subway has also used Hulu to present its series "4 to 9ers" about teens and young adults and their antics in this fast-food establishment. YouTube is another popular outlet for these series. Maybelline has a series called "Vanity" and AT&T produces "Summer Break," which it also puts on Tumblr and Twitter.

Content can also be quite simple. The best example here is Blendtec. The blender company didn't have a lot of money to spend on advertising so it wanted to do something to grab people's attention. This led to a series of videos showing all manner of items—from an iPad to a golf club—being pulverized by the blender. These have become some of the most watched videos online.

Beyond the digital realm, marketers are creating content to appear in more traditional television formats. Pennzoil produced a documentary called "Breaking Barriers" about breaking the speed limit, and GE produced a series about scientific breakthroughs, both of which aired on the National Geographic cable channel.

Is there a way to spot content marketing?

There are a couple of things to look for that will help you identify content marketing. First, most content marketing is video-based. People are reading less, certainly less long-form content. We are easily attracted by videos, especially on mobile devices. Marketers attempt to attract us through short videos that can be optimized through social media. Once we click on the link, then we get the longer videos outlined above. This format is particularly appealing to marketers because videos cannot be blocked by ad blockers. Not all content marketing is video, but the trend is moving in that direction as marketers can more easily track video on mobile.

Another element to look for is that the story will present the customer as the hero rather than the product. This is fundamental to how marketers become friends with us: they stroke our egos. In the example above, Intel includes either people or their artwork in its films. In another example, camera maker GoPro posts videos created by its users. While the company used to be sports-focused, it has now broadened the content to include categories like music and furry friends in order to widen its audience. "Fireman Saves Kitten" is one of the most popular GoPro videos of all time. An *Ad Age* winner for "Best User-Created Viral Ad," this video (created with the GoPro camera) shows a fireman rescuing a kitten by pouring water over him and placing an oxygen mask over his face. What makes this really interesting is that the user is the hero and the video wasn't initially created as an ad. Moreover, making the fireman—or, more broadly, us—the hero pushes the product toward the margins of the marketing. We don't see the GoPro camera; we see what it does. Same with Intel. We don't see the computer process; we see the imagination that it is supposed to inspire within us. Content marketing is about stories, not selling.

Finally, marketers are looking to evoke an emotion so they can make a connection. This is why stories are so important. When we become immersed in the characters' lives, we are transported. This happens as the tension builds throughout a narrative. The one we are most familiar with is the universal story structure—first, there's a surprise, followed by obstacles that build to a climax; then, the protagonist looks within to overcome the adversity; and finally resolution. This hero's story is widely used by marketers. As we become engaged in the story, we will stick with it because we want to know what happens, and we become emotionally invested.[29]

Are there other forms of stealth marketing we might not be aware of?

There are any number of sponsored messages that we see that are not designated as advertising. Notable among these are sponsored tweets where a celebrity is paid to promote a product, only without the "promoted" notation on the site. Blog posts mention products without divulging that the writer was paid for the placement. Same holds true for Instagram and YouTube, where influencers with large followings post a picture containing an advertiser's product or create a video review touting its benefits, all without indicating that a sponsor is involved.

Is social media connected to the success of this format?

Social media are fundamental to the spread of these forms of stealth marketing. BuzzFeed, for example, gets 75 percent of its readers through social media—it's not about getting people to the site, it's about getting the company's content distributed on Facebook, which has more than 1.6 billion users.

First, it was not the Internet alone that led to the rise in digital advertising; companies had been able to produce websites for almost two decades. The problem was that they couldn't get consumers to go to the site unless there was something they wanted to buy, like Amazon, or a search engine, like Google. Social media created a reason for people to send corporate messages from one person to another.

29. Paul Zak (October 28, 2014), "Why Your Brain Loves Good Storytelling," *Harvard Business Review*. Retrieved July 1, 2015 from https://hbr.org/2014/10/why-your-brain-loves-good-storytelling/.

Second, we have been trained to think of social media sites as places of community. We amass "friends" and we "share" the best information with them. Facebook wants us to think that the site is about showing our latest baby pictures, but it's really about how it can sell you the next toy or diaper or other baby item you need. And when Facebook isn't serving up the ads, we are. See a cute listicle on BuzzFeed and you send it to your friends. Or you send that adorable ad with the animals from Android.

Social media are the newest tool for implementing word-of-mouth (WOM) marketing. WOM marketing is defined as "the technique of promoting a product, service or business by soliciting positive comments from satisfied customers. Word of mouth marketing is an interactive process such that customers are collaborating with the business, product, or service for which they have derived enough satisfaction that they are willing to speak out about it and even recommend it to others." Through social media, marketers ask us to talk about their products and typically provide something to us in return, whether it is a coupon or the possibility of winning a prize for participating in a contest. Influencers, on the other hand, receive either free product or payments. Advertisers have long known that this is the best form of marketing because people believe their friends when they endorse something. According to Nielsen's *Trust in Advertising* report, 84 percent of respondents say WOM is the most trustworthy form of advertising. The communication started with the marketer, but by the time your friend sends you the post, that connection is not readily visible.

The popularity of mobile devices is driving the increased use of WOM marketing. We can comment, read, and post on the go. Americans already spend more time on mobile devices than watching television, which means that advertisers are moving there, too. They are mostly on the apps where we spend our time—Google Maps, Facebook, YouTube, Pandora, and Gmail. These five apps account for 80 percent of our time on mobile.

On average, 75 percent of Americans talk about brands daily, they typically mention ten brands, and 70 percent of the time a recommendation is part of the conversation. Some of those recommendations are simply part of everyday conversation: "Have you tried that new Frappuccino at Starbucks?" or "Target is having a great summer sale." This is unsponsored WOM marketing. When brands intervene, that is sponsored WOM, and it can go by a number of different names, including viral marketing and buzz marketing.

The point, though, is to make these communications feel as if there is no corporate influence. The way to do this is by finding influencers to talk about the brand. With their many friends and followers, the expectation is that the conversation will go viral. The Word of Mouth Marketing Association (WOMMA) defines buzz marketing as the use of "high-profile entertainment or news to get people to talk about your brand," and this, of course, means social media. There are a couple of ways companies can make this happen. One is to pay for celebrity tweets and posts. Top stars can get tens of thousands of dollars for 140 characters or for being pictured with a product. The other way is to pay people to blog about or review a product without mentioning that they have been paid to do so. This is illegal, but it still happens. Amazon's Vine program provides products for free to "trusted reviewers." Companies, notably Izea and Ad.ly, connect bloggers with products and offer compensation for including a product on a blog post or an Instagram, just like product placement in other media.

Finally, companies run contests asking people to create a video or post a picture, and then they tap into consumers' use of social media. The annual Doritos Super Bowl ad is one example. Another example is Coca-Cola's "Share a Coke," a campaign where bottles of Coke, Diet Coke, and Coke Zero had labels that bore 250 of the most common first names, as well as a few titles like Mom and BFF. People readily took pictures of themselves with their soda cans and posted them online. Budweiser used the same strategy with its #upforanything campaign, and Intel integrated social aspects into all of its Inside films.

The goal in all of this, of course, is for the advertising to go viral.

Why does some content go viral?

Instead of talking with our neighbors over the backyard fence, today we are compelled to share via social media. And instead of talking with one person, we are talking to a few hundred, if we consider that the median number of friends on Facebook is 200. That isn't a lot, but if a handful of those people pass on the message, and then some of their friends pass on a message, it can scale up pretty quickly. If the message reaches more than a thousand people, according to social media company Lithium, it can "generate up to 1/2 million conversations about your brand." To help ensure that happens, marketers find and usually compensate influencers, who can generate up to five times more WOM messages than you or I could. In addition, messages sent from influencers are four times more likely to sway purchase decisions.

But what actually motives us to share a video or an article with our friends? Jonah Berger, a Wharton professor, writes in his book *Contagious* that content goes viral because of one or more of the following factors: Social Currency, Triggers, Emotion, Public, Practical Value, and Stories. Nothing about this is earth-shatteringly new. Social currency is about being up on the latest topic. It's why *People* magazine was invented. If you know something before someone else, like how to get tickets to *Hamilton* or who did an awesome lip sync on *The Tonight Show Starring Jimmy Fallon*, that can give you standing in a group. Triggers are reminders in our environment. In traditional media, that would be an outdoor ad. White earbuds send our minds to thinking about Apple. We have all been moved by some form of online content, whether it was to laugh at the Ice Bucket Challenge or cry at Dove "Sketches" or get really mad at KONY2012. These emotions, the most common of which are awe and anger, drive us to act. Next is making the private public. That was what Livestrong bracelets did for cancer charities. Practical value has to do with sharing content that people find useful, such as recipe videos or how-to makeup sites. Finally, people like stories. We don't connect to things; we connect to ideas, which are conveyed through narratives. If those stories resonate with us, we are more likely to pass them on.

An example helps illustrate the point. The most viewed ad in 2014 was a video called "First Kiss." In this black-and-white video, strangers were introduced in a bare studio and asked to kiss for the first time. The couples were gay and straight, young and old. This concept was incredibly compelling: How do you start kissing someone you've just met? As far as watching the video, the obvious question of why someone would produce this film to begin with has to enter your mind. There is no indication that this is an ad other than a title that says "WREN presents" that appears for a few seconds at the beginning. "FIRST KISS a film by Tatia Pilieva" next appears, which signals that this is artistic work and not advertising. Since most people did not know Wren was an apparel company, the line at the beginning was not helpful in alerting people to its commercial aspect. While more than 150 million people viewed the video, not all of them were happy about it.[30]

The importance of tapping into emotions is key and is being used by advertisers in ways that wouldn't have been used in the past. A current ad shows moms talking to an off-screen interviewer about how much they care about their children. One mother even says, "I've heard people say that your child is your heart walking," which she can barely say because she

30. Eric Dodds (March 12, 2014), "Why That 'First Kiss' Video Now Feels Like A Bad First Date," *Time.com*. Retrieved May 27, 2016 from http://time.com/21332/why-that-first-kiss-video-now-feels-like-a-bad-first-date/.

wells up in tears. This is not an ad for Pampers; it is for carpet cleaning!

What is real-time marketing?

The best example of real-time marketing is the "Dunk in the Dark" ad from Oreo. During Super Bowl XLVII, the lights went out at the Super Dome. While people waited for illumination to return, Oreo created an ad on the spot—that is, in real time—showing the cookie coming into frame with the background in black and the area partially lit. Oreo was able to do this only because it was in the midst of a 100-day-long campaign in which the cookie was tied to cultural events from Pride Day to Elvis's birthday.

Other marketers continue to try and replicate this. The Samsung Oscar selfie with Ellen DeGeneres comes close, and numerous marketers jumped on the royal baby bandwagon. Given this, look for marketers to attempt real-time ads during big events, which will generate more sharing.

But why do we share?

Sometimes we share because of motivation from the marketer, whether it's to get a coupon for posting something online or because we've entered a contest and might win a million dollars.

But we also share for personal reasons—notably, we want to connect with others. Part and parcel of this is managing our image. We might be trying to project an image of helpfulness by forwarding a recipe video, or we might want to appear philanthropic so we "like" a charity that marries up with our concerns. Some of the people we end up connecting with are marketers, and they develop their campaigns to foster this interaction, as noted previously.

The other part of sharing is about sharing our feelings, something well noted by Berger and others. BuzzFeed taps into this by providing lightweight content for the "bored at work network," millennials stuck at their desk during lunch who are looking for a laugh to share with friends. Facebook took advantage of this by running its emotional contagion experiment in the summer of 2014. Knowing that people pass feelings, Facebook manipulated the newsfeeds of 689,003 people to see if increasing negative information would make them sadder; it did.[31] Social media combined with emotional manipulation thus leads to videos going viral.

Can we share too much?

Indeed, we can be overexposed, and many people do overshare (read: Donald Trump), but it may not be our fault.

The statistics tell the story. Facebook has 1.44 billion users, Twitter has 284 million, and Instagram, Pinterest, and LinkedIn have 300, 40, and 364 million respectively. Those numbers have grown because of what is known as *network effects*. As more people become part of the network, it increases in value. Then it gets to the point where it is harder *not* to be part of the social media network, especially when the media or your friends are talking about this or that video being the hottest thing on Facebook or the trending topic on Twitter. Once on the sites, we learn the norms from watching what our friends do, and sites like Facebook capitalize on peer pressure to emulate others. Twenty-four percent of American Facebook users feel pressured to overshare, according to Pew Research.

Technology also feeds oversharing. Most people do not know how to use privacy settings correctly and end up sharing with the public by default, instead of with only their close friends. Notifications bring us back to our devices again and

31. Gregory S. McNeal (June 28, 2014), "Facebook Manipulated User News Feeds to Create Emotional Responses," *Forbes*. Retrieved February 17, 2015 from http://www.forbes.com/sites/gregorymcneal/2014/06/28/facebook-manipulated-user-news-feeds-to-create-emotional-contagion/.

again to check in, if only to leave a comment on someone else's post. This is no accident: the social networks have been devised to create perpetual communication. Some of this is through technology but some of it is in the language used with social media. On Facebook we are part of a "community" where we have "friends" with whom we want to "share." These word choices are no fluke. Israeli researcher Nicholas John notes "the spread of the notion of sharing lies in its positive connotations of equality, selflessness, and giving, in combination with its resonance with what is viewed as the proper mode of communication between intimates. In brief, sharing is associated with positive social relations, as expressed through the popular phrase, 'sharing and caring,' which has been appropriated by SNSs [social network sites] to infuse their services with the positive implications of that term."[32] The more we share the better we feel, even if what we share is corporate-sponsored content.

What is the connection between social media and customer relationship marketing?

From the marketer's perspective, social media are all about creating a long-term relationship with consumers or prospective consumers, what is known as customer relationship marketing (CRM), which we looked at in the previous chapter. Whereas the traditional relationship between us and brands might be a commercial and then a purchase at a store, that is no longer the case. Part of that has to do with experiential marketing and now social media, which now allows direct one-to-one relationships with consumers.

What I heard from marketers over and over again in my research was "social is not for selling, it's for social." They use social media in a number of ways to create those relationships.

32. Nicholas A. John (2012), "Sharing and Web 2.0: The Emergence of a Keyword," *New Media and Society*. Retrieved May 23, 2016 from http://nms.sagepub.com/content/early/2012/07/03/1461444812450684.

The "like" button on Facebook, for example, allows us to show others what we care about. It also enables the brand to engage with us. In a particularly witty version of this, Groupon posted a product called the banana bunker. Knowing this product would spark numerous innuendoes, the company responded with a quip to anyone who posted a comment with sexual overtones. Thousands of consumers were thoroughly entertained while the product got lots of (free) press coverage and sold out in two hours.

Another way that marketers interact with consumers is through real-time listening. In this popular technique advertisers "listen" online to see how consumers are talking about the brand. One company that is particularly adept at using social media in this way is Purina. Members of its marketing department will find out that an animal has had surgery and will contact the pet owner to make sure everything is okay—not once but perhaps multiple times. Or, they watch online to see when they can inject the brand into a social conversation. Laura Spica, a typical dog owner, posted a picture on Twitter of her pet looking out the window at squirrels. Purina tweeted back the dog's picture after having drawn in a hat, sunglasses, a jacket, and a badge with the words, "Squirrel Patrol." The dog owner tweeted back: @Purina Oh-Em-Gee! You pimped my #PurinaDog! That's possibly the cutest thing I've ever seen!!! #SquirrelPatrol #HenryDog. Thus, Ms. Spica becomes a spokesperson for Purina in a little under a minute.

How is this affecting advertising on legacy media?

In Chapter 2, we talked about NBC reducing its commercial load on *Saturday Night Live* in order to provide more time for content. However, the additional content would include brand integration (i.e., advertising). NBC is doing this because it has already had some initial success with this strategy. We can expect other networks to implement this as well if advertisers like it and consumers don't complain.

We see this happening more fully at CNN, which announced in 2015 that it was forming an in-house studio expressly to produce advertising that appears to be news. The studio, called Courageous, is staffed with journalists and filmmakers who report to an executive who used to work at Ogilvy & Mather, a major advertising agency. While I have yet to see examples of this in the United States, the network provides examples of how it has implemented branded content overseas. For Sofitel, for example, it created a campaign around Paris Fashion Season. The campaign included television content made up of two weeks of daily segments (one in spring and one in fall), vignettes about Paris (one can assume with shots of Sofitel hotels), a thirty-minute program, and a co-branded television promotion. There was also an online element with banner ads and a dedicated Fashion Season section that was solely promoted by the hotelier. And, finally, the campaign got trade and consumer press coverage as well as "Social Media pushes from CNN International."[33]

What are the consequences of digital advertising on content?

The ever-increasing move of advertising dollars out of television and print and into digital has had serious downsides for the media, and more importantly for us.

As digital increased, newspapers were not nimble enough to pivot, and papers that had been in business for 150 years or more went out of business. For others, it has meant allowing for more native advertising and other content forms that blur the line between sponsored content and unbiased editorial: the ultimate crumbling of the wall between church and state (editorial and advertising). In the past, journalists would have fought tooth and nail to keep advertisers out, but today

33. CNN (n.d). Commercial Case Studies (*Sofitel: Fashion Season: Paris*). Retrieved May 10, 2016 from http://commercial.cnn.com/case-studies/fashion-season/.

they cannot afford to do so. Instead of recognizable ads next to an article, the article itself is the ad. Worse for us, it is almost impossible to tell which is which.

The same is true for television. Morning news shows are cluttered with segments that are barely veiled advertising. Product placement has proliferated. And now, networks are cutting down the number of commercials so they can allow for more branded sponsorship within the program itself.

While we cannot know what the endgame will be, we can speculate that the quality of content will continue to decrease, first because of the impinging commercialization and then because so much advertising has moved out of legacy media that the companies will not have the funds to produce the kind of programming we have come to expect. So if advertising is becoming less and less expensive and the only thing that people can afford to produce with less revenue is cat memes and low-quality video content, then better-quality content will have to be paid for by subscription.

Is this the end of the free Internet?

Yes. If advertising is no longer the means for funding media content, the alternative is subscriptions. Think here of HBO; people pay for the programming so they do not need to watch commercials. This is the direction that television is headed as more and more producers create over-the-top (OTT) television options, such as Showtime Anytime or CBS Access, which are apps that allow you to get this programming without being attached to a cable provider. Cord cutters and cord nevers (those who have stopped subscribing to cable or those who never have) are on the rise. This has major consequences for the basic cable networks such as MTV, CNN, FX, Nickelodeon, and so on, because they derive a considerable percentage of their revenue from payments from cable operators. As people start paying for individual subscriptions (to Netflix, Hulu, HBO Now, and so on), cable subscriptions will continue to decline, while your monthly entertainment bill is likely to increase.

The same will hold true for the Internet. If we all become smart enough to avoid advertising or the advertising revenue drops precipitously (which is likely, because no one is watching the ads), then expect to pay out of pocket for the content you've been getting for free.

What is the future of advertising apt to look like?

If I had been asked this question thirty years ago, the answer would have been simple: advertising will continue to appear on television, in newspapers and magazines, on radio, and on billboards. Today, advertising is in the most dynamic period ever, and I'm not the only one who thinks so. When conducting research, I used to ask practitioners where they see the industry going in five years. Then, I changed the question to two years. Finally, my interviewees said they could only speculate what might happen in the next six months—things are changing that quickly.

Here's my best guess. Television will continue to be an important medium. I say this because most online producers are looking to create more video, and now they are admitting that they really want their work to be on television and not the third screen.[34] Advertising will partially support the medium, but it will continue to be integrated into the content, or consumers might even be paid to watch advertising. Those that can afford it will pay not to see the ads. Expect, too, more crossover between digital and legacy media, such as NBCUniversal's investment in BuzzFeed and Vox. Sadly, more newspapers will fold, but the medium will not disappear altogether. Just as people are returning to physical books, there will still be an

34. Jeremy Barr (August 2, 2016), "Digital Media Companies Continue Slow March Toward TV," *Advertising Age*. Retrieved August 17, 2016 from http://adage.com/article/media/digital-media-companies-continue-march-television/305204/.

audience for physical newspapers. Advertising in this medium will continue to move toward the native advertising variety. Digital will move increasingly to mobile, and new technologies will improve on the cookie in order to track us while we are on the go. Augmented reality apps, like Pokémon GO, will proliferate, and new online/offline advertising experiences will appear. Virtual reality will evolve, enabling consumers to have numerous commercial experiences without leaving their home. Marketers' access to our information will increase as the Internet of Things explodes and our Fitbits, refrigerators, cars, and baby monitors are all connected to the Internet, allowing companies to track our every move, calorie, and heartbeat.

We can all hope that this is for the good. The most positive among us envision a world where we will see advertising only for products and services that are of interest to us; that data will enable our every want and need to be predicted, from when we need a cup of coffee to when our gas tanks need refilling; and that when advertising does appear, it will contain information that helps to improve our existence.[35] I'm not so sanguine. Just like digital marketers really want to be in television, advertisers want consumers to know they are behind the content. It runs counter to their DNA—and to capitalism, frankly—so it couldn't be any other way.

35. Brian Wong (April 26, 2015), "The Future of Advertising: Farewell, Mass Marketing," *Wall Street Journal*. Retrieved August 17, 2016 from http://www.wsj.com/articles/the-future-of-advertising-farewell-mass-marketing-1430105034.

APPENDIX

Additional resources for those researching advertising, or if you simply want to learn more:

Advertising Industry Publications: Publications that cover broad aspects of the advertising industry.

Advertising Age—www.adage.com

Adweek—www.adweek.com

Brandweek—http://www.adweek.com/topic/brand week-report

Marketing News—https://www.ama.org/publications/Market ingNews/Pages/Current-Issue.aspx

Media Industry Publications: Magazines and websites that report on the latest topics related to individual media, such as television, magazines, or digital.

Broadcasting & Cable—www.broadcastingcable.com

Folio—www.foliomag.com

Mediapost—http://www.mediapost.com/

MIN/Media Industry Newsletter—www.minonline.com

Multichannel News—http://www.multichannel.com/

Variety—www.variety.com

Academic Journals: Leading scholarly publications in the areas of media, advertising, and marketing. (Note: I do not provide web addresses for many of these publications because they may only be available if you are associated with an academic institution that subscribes to it. I provide them here as reference for the top publications in the field.)

Association for Education in Journalism and Mass Communication—www.aejmc.org. (This organization publishes a number of journals, which you can find on its site. Also, I specifically cite this group because it has an advertising division.)

Critical Studies in Media Communication

Harvard Business Review—https://hbr.org/

Journal of Advertising

Journal of Advertising Research—http://www.journalofadvertisingresearch.com/

Journal of Broadcasting and Electronic Media

Journal of Business Research

Journal of Communication

Journal of Consumer Research

Journal of Marketing

Journal of Marketing Research

Journal of Mass Media Ethics

Marketing Science—http://pubsonline.informs.org/toc/mksc/current

New Media & Society

Associations: Theses organizations provide extensive information about advertising, marketing, media, or all three. Most websites contain industry or academic research as well as opportunities to attend events with industry leaders, either as a member or not. For those interested in working in the industry, several of these associations have student or young professional memberships and mentoring opportunities.

Advertising Club of New York—http://www.theadvertisingclub.org/

The Advertising Council, Inc.—www.adcouncil.org

Advertising Research Foundation—www.arfsite.org

Advertising Women of New York—awny.org

American Advertising Foundation—www.aaf.org

American Association of Advertising Agencies—www.aaaa.org

American Marketing Association—www.marketingpower.com

Association of Consumer Research—www.acrwebsite.org

Association of National Advertisers—www.ana.net

Center for Communication—http://www.centerforcommunication.org/

Direct Marketing Association, Inc.—www.the-dma.org

Interactive Advertising Bureau (IAB)—http://www.iab.com/

Magazine Publishers of America—www.magazine.org

National Academy of Television Arts and Sciences (The Emmys)—http://emmyonline.org/

New York NATAS—http://www.nyemmys.org/

NCTA—The Internet & Television Association—www.ncta.com

Newspaper Association of America—http://cms.naa.org

Public Relations Society of America—www.prsa.org

Television Bureau of Advertising—www.tvb.org

Video Advertising Bureau—http://www.thevab.com/

Government Organizations: The two main governmental bodies responsible for overseeing this area.

Federal Communications Commission—www.fcc.gov

Federal Trade Commission—https://www.ftc.gov/

Historical Sites: Select list of museum and research websites that provide historical information about advertising and media.

The Hartman Center for Sales, Advertising, and Marketing History—http://library.duke.edu/rubenstein/hartman/index.html

Media History Digital Library—http://mediahistoryproject.org/

Museum of Brands, Packaging, and Advertising—http://
www.museumofbrands.com/

Museum of the Moving Image—http://www.movingim-
age.us/

The Museum of Public Relations—www.prmuseum.com/
bernays/bernays_1929a.html

The Paley Center for Media (formerly The Museum of
Television & Radio)—https://media.paleycenter.org/

Research and Information Services: Leading research companies and institutions. Most of these sites have research available for free to the public.

Advertising Red Books (Standard Directory of Advertising
Agencies)

Alliance for Audited Media (formerly Audit Bureau of
Circulation)

eMarketer—https://www.emarketer.com/

Forrester—https://go.forrester.com

Gallup & Robinson—www.gallup-robinson.com

Media Effects Research Lab at Pennsylvania State
University—www.psu.edu/dept/medialab

Media Industries Project—http://www.carseywolf.ucsb.
edu/mip/1

Mediamark Research—www.mediamark.com

The Nielsen Company—http://www.nielsen.com/us/en.
html

Pew Internet and American Life Project—www.pewinter-
net.org/

Trendwatching—http://trendwatching.com/

Advocacy Groups: Organizations that criticize advertising
and commercialization, and fight for media reform.

Campaign for a Commercial Free Childhood—http://
www.commercialfreechildhood.org/

Center for Media Literacy—www.medialit.org

The Electronic Frontier Foundation—www.eff.org

Foolproof—http://www.foolproofme.com/

FreePress.net—www.freepress.net

Media Education Foundation—www.mediaed.org

Media Smarts—http://mediasmarts.ca/

New York Women in Film & Television (NYWIFT)—
http://nywift.org/

The Norman Lear Center—http://blog.learcenter.org/

Select Advertising Agencies and Holding Companies:

360i—https://360i.com/

72andSunny—https://www.72andsunny.com/

Crispin Porter + Bogusky—http://www.cpbgroup.com/

Dentsu—http://www.dentsu.com/

Droga5—http://droga5.com/

Interpublic Group—https://www.interpublic.com/

The Martin Agency—http://www.martinagency.com/

OmnicomGroup—www.omnicomgroup.com

Publicis Worldwide—http://www.publicis.com/

TBWA Chiat Day—http://tbwachiatday.com/

Weiden + Kennedy—http://www.wk.com/

WPP—http://www.wpp.com/wpp/

INDEX